Mike Schmidt
Baseball's
King of Swing

Mike Schmidt Baseball's King of Swing

by
STAN HOCHMAN
illustrated with photographs

A Zander Hollander Sports Book
RANDOM HOUSE NEW YORK

To my wife, Gloria, an award-winning medical writer, and my daughter, Anndee, editor-in-chief of the Yale *Daily News*, who have made me very proud while making me the third-best writer in the family.

Copyright © 1983 by Associated Features Inc. All rights reserved under International and Pan-American Copyright Conventions. Published in the United States by Random House, Inc., New York, and simultaneously in Canada by Random House of Canada Limited, Toronto.

Library of Congress Cataloging in Publication Data:

Hochman, Stan.
    Mike Schmidt: baseball's king of swing.

"A Zander Hollander sports book."

SUMMARY: A biography of the star third baseman of the Philadelphia Phillies who was the third National Leaguer ever chosen Most Valuable Player for two years in a row.

    1. Schmidt, Mike, [date]—Juvenile literature.   2. Baseball players—United States—Biography—Juvenile literature.   3. Philadelphia Phillies (Baseball team)—Juvenile literature.   [1. Schmidt, Mike.   2. Baseball players]   I. Title.
GV865.S36H62   1983   796.357'092'4   [B]   [92]   83-4529
ISBN: 0-394-85806-9 (pbk.)

PHOTOGRAPH CREDITS: The Lois and Jack Schmidt Collection, pages, 2, 10, 14, 16, 20; the Philadelphia Phillies, pages 47, 113, 122; United Press International, pages viii, 56, 63, 65, 81, 96, 108, 110.

Manufactured in the United States of America   1 2 3 4 5 6 7 8 9 0

Acknowledgments

I would like to thank Mike Schmidt for his patience and cooperation. And I would like to acknowledge the help provided by Donna Schmidt, Mike's wife, and by Jack and Lois Schmidt, Mike's parents. Also former Ohio University coach Jack Wren and Phillies' scout Tony Lucadello; Phillies' publicists Larry Shenk and Chris Wheeler; Philadelphia *Daily News* sports editor Mike Rathet for allowing me the flexibility to do this project; and Zander Hollander for having faith in a first-time author.

—STAN HOCHMAN

Contents

	Introduction	ix
1.	A Shocking Start	3
2.	Weak in the Knees	8
3.	A Switch in Time	15
4.	Around the Horn	22
5.	Minor Leagues, Major Problems	31
6.	"Dutch"	39
7.	An All-Star Surprise	46
8.	"Captain Cool"	58
9.	A Look in the Mirror	71
10.	Getting Ready	80
11.	Leap Year	91
12.	Most Valuable Lessons	107
13.	On the Right Track	121

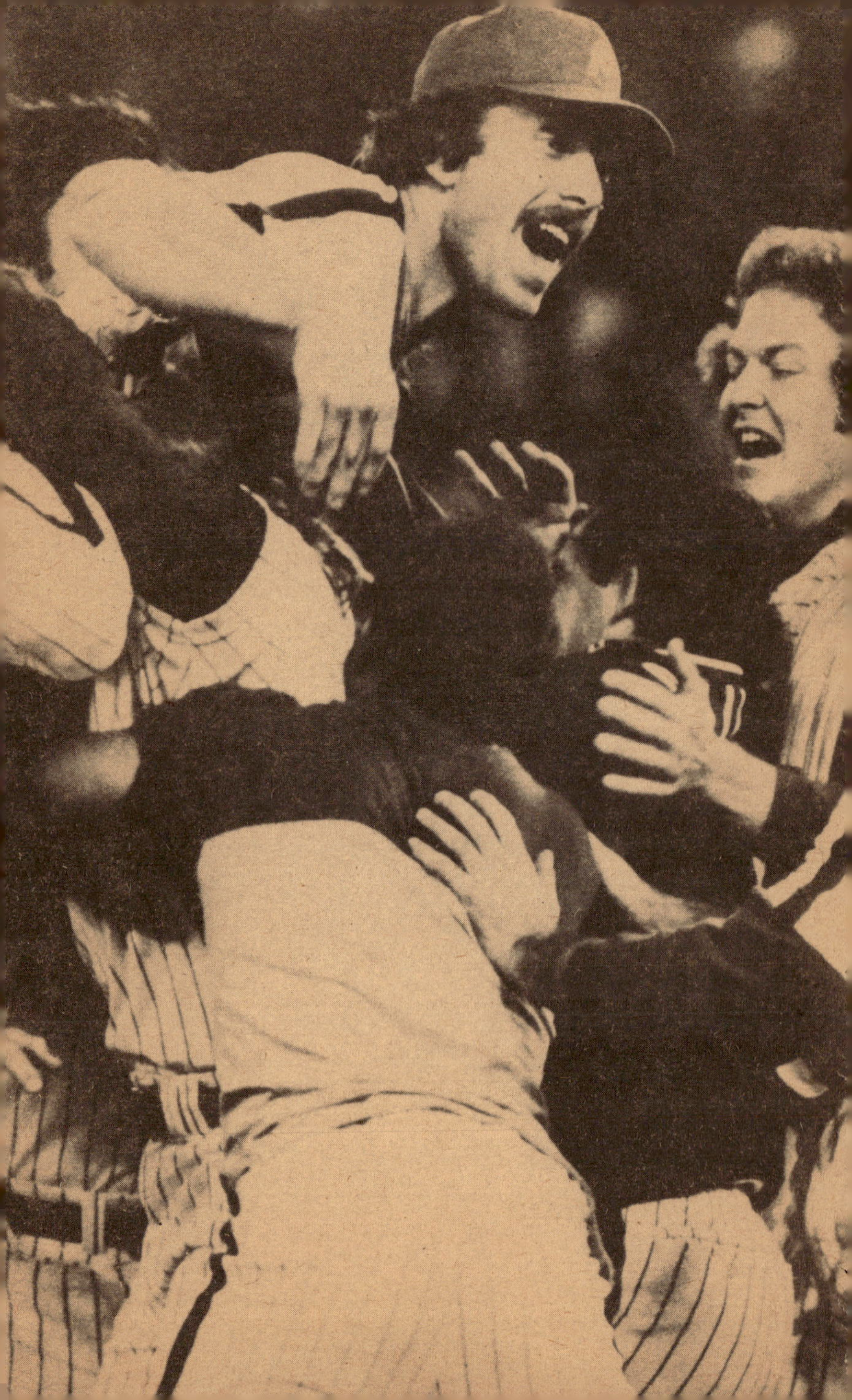

Introduction

It was a World Series game like no other World Series game. In Philadelphia's Veterans Stadium outfield were mounted policemen wearing riot helmets, their nervous horses pawing at the artificial turf. Near the box seats stood more cops, with snarling dogs straining at leashes.

And on the mound was Tug McGraw trying to pitch the Philadelphia Phillies to their first world championship. The Phillies held a 4–1 lead, but Kansas City had loaded the bases with one out.

McGraw sighed deeply, and then got Frank White to pop a foul ball near the Phillies' dugout. Bob Boone camped under it. The ball plopped into Boone's glove and then, like a bar of slippery soap, squirted out of it. But there was Pete Rose, hustling alongside, to catch the ball. Two out.

The next hitter was Willie Wilson, who had struck out 11 times during the Series. The count went to 1-2, and then McGraw reached back and threw a fastball. Wilson swung and missed.

The 1980 World Series was over. The Phillies had won. The fans shrieked in the stands, unable to pour onto the field because of the police. That left the stage to the players.

Boone wobbled out, on battered legs, to embrace McGraw. A mob formed at the mound, joyful Phillies running out from under their hats to join the celebration.

And then, from third base, came Mike Schmidt, whooping and hollering. Five feet from the swarm of teammates, he jumped, like a swimmer starting an Olympic race. He covered those last five feet parallel to the ground, landing atop the pile of humanity.

Mike Schmidt? Unflappable Mike Schmidt in an emotional display? Mike Schmidt the Most Valuable Player in the World Series after hitting .381 with two homers and seven runs batted in?

Was this the same Mike Schmidt who had hit a wretched .196 in his rookie season? The same Mike Schmidt who was often criticized for being too nonchalant, too cool?

Yes, it was the same Mike Schmidt who had scuffled back from that first woeful season in the league to win back-to-back MVP awards, to lead the major leagues in home runs five times, to win the Gold Glove for fielding excellence seven times.

He had battled back, against a mob of doubters, to become the best player in baseball, the king of swing. And this is his story.

Mike Schmidt
Baseball's
King of Swing

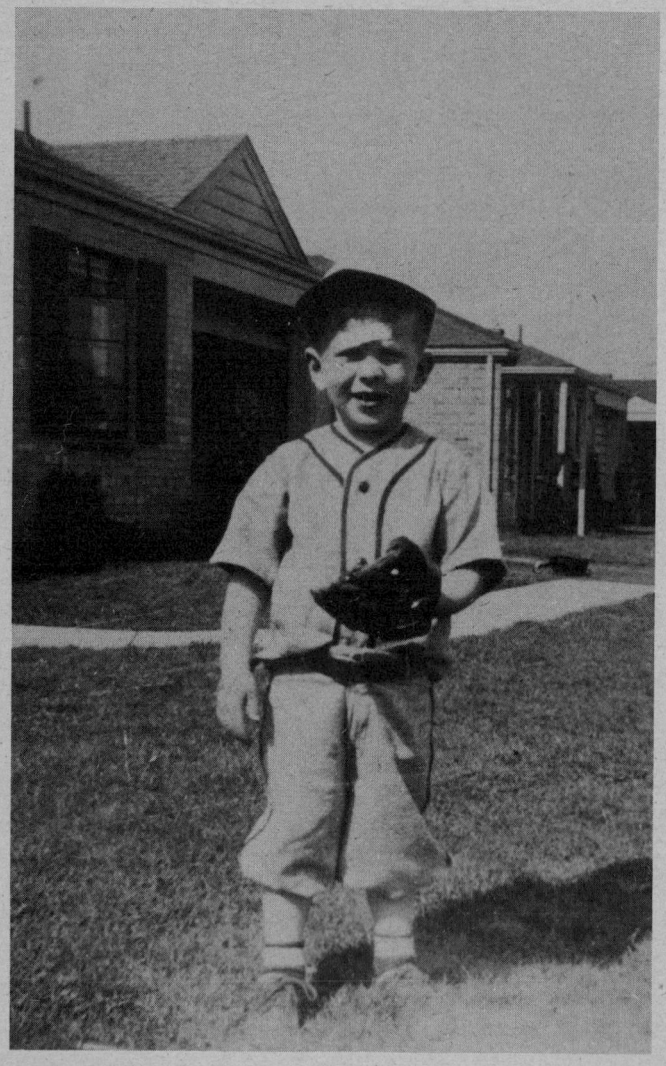

Mike was only three and a half years old when the family camera captured him in front of the Schmidts' home in Dayton, Ohio.

1

A Shocking Start

He was four years old. Freckle-faced. Red hair. The kind of face they use on the front of cereal boxes now to show how much kids love their contents.

He was wearing a baseball uniform that had once belonged to his dad. "A & A Grill" it said in faded lettering. But the shirt was now so small that one "A" was under his right armpit.

He was swinging a regulation Little League bat, holding it down at the end, with only the knob showing beneath knuckles turning white with tension.

The pitcher stood 15 feet away. The pitcher was a tiny woman with strawberry-blonde hair that glittered in the afternoon sun. She threw the ball underhand, a Wiffle ball that floated toward the little boy like a balloon.

When she let go of the ball, the boy scowled, chewing his lower lip. And when the ball got close, he swung at it, grinding his heels into the soft grass.

"I swung hard," Mike Schmidt recalled years later. "I've always swung hard."

Michael Jack Schmidt was born on September 27, 1949, in Dayton, Ohio, and grew up there. His father, Jack, worked for a linen supply company. His mother, Lois, worked at a swimming pool her family owned. His grandmother, Viola Schmidt, often baby-sat.

She had cut down Jack Schmidt's old A & A Grill baseball shirt to fit her grandson. She enjoyed tucking him into the shirt and going into the backyard to pitch to him, watching him swing from the heels at her soft tosses.

When Mike was five, Jack Schmidt left the linen supply job to operate Jack's Drive-In, a fast-food restaurant next to the family-owned swimming pool, the Phillips Aquatic Club. The Schmidts moved to North Dayton, to a house on Pinecrest Drive, with an impressive old ash tree in the backyard.

Mike Schmidt climbed that tree almost every day, scrambling up a cyclone fence until he could grab the lowest branch, then shinny up the trunk.

One August day, when he was seven, he tugged on a pair of brand-new sneakers. His grandparents were on a vacation trip, his dad was at work, and his mom had some errands to run. She hired a neighborhood teenager to baby-sit.

"Michael, those are brand-new sneakers," his mother lectured before leaving. "Now, don't you get them all scuffed and dirty the very first day."

His mother was barely out of the driveway before Mike headed for the tempting ash tree. The baby sitter watched, amused, as the boy disappeared into the leafy tangle.

"Higher," she called. "Let's see how high you can go."

That was music to a seven-year-old boy's ears. Mike scrambled onto branches he had never reached before, panting with the excitement that comes from exploring uncharted territory.

And then, about 24 feet above the ground, he groped for a sturdy branch and found only thin twigs. The tree seemed to be swaying and he felt the need to grab on to something, anything, to maintain his balance.

There was a wire he had seen from the lower

branches. He stretched for it, clutching it in his right hand. Zapppppp!

Mike Schmidt felt the surge of 4,000 volts of electricity pulsing into his quivering body. Stunned by the shock, he toppled forward. The branch he was standing on cracked and the boy began to fall, crashing from branch to branch until he hit the ground with a thud. The baby sitter screamed in fear. Mike got to his knees groggily, then to his feet. He wobbled toward the house while the baby sitter ran in search of help.

Neighbors came sprinting into the backyard and found Mike staggering to the back steps. The scent of burned flesh was in the air as they bundled him into a car for a swift trip to the hospital.

He had been scorched in the palm of his right hand where the electricity had entered and on his right shin where it had left.

If he hadn't been wearing those new sneakers, he might have been electrocuted. The rubber soles saved his life by grounding the current.

The neighbors summoned Mike's mother to the hospital and she took him home. For the next two months she applied ointment to the burned areas three times a day.

The scars of that close call remain—a thin white line on his right hand, an apple-sized red blotch on his right shin. And so do the memories.

2

Weak in the Knees

Getting jolted by 4,000 volts of electricity and toppling out of the upper branches of an ash tree didn't slow Mike Schmidt down. The following spring he showed up at the North Dayton Little League tryouts.

They pinned a number to the back of his shirt and hit grounders to him. They nodded at his sure hands. They pitched to him and watched him lash at the ball. They grinned at his big, ferocious swing.

Ordinarily, eight-year-olds played tee-ball— they hit baseballs propped on a rubber tee instead of facing live pitchers. But Mike seemed so smooth, so sure of himself, that the manager of the J. M. Skelton team "drafted" him for his ballclub. He stuck Mike at third base to take advantage of his strong arm.

In one of Mike's first games, while his father watched from the bleachers, there was a tough play at third. A runner was trying to advance from second on a groundball to the shortstop.

Mike crouched, waiting for the throw. The ball arrived, and so did the 12-year-old runner—feet first. When the dust cleared, Mike Schmidt was on his back, four feet behind the base. His dad's worried frown turned to a proud grin when he saw that Mike was still clutching the baseball. The youngster had the determination to go with his quick hands and strong arm.

When the Little League season ended, Mike and the neighborhood kids played pickup games at Ridgecrest Playground.

"We played in one corner of the field," Schmidt remembered. "There was a gully in right field. So, if you hit the ball to right, it was an automatic out. That probably explains why I still hit the ball to left, even now."

The kids always kept score but they sometimes lost track of time. Hunger took a backseat to another turn at bat. Most nights, Mike would take that one last swing before heeding his mother's dinner call. And one night, caught up in the excitement of a ballgame, he ignored a second call and a third.

Mike finally trudged home, sweaty and tired. As he shuffled into the back door he heard a yelp of anger at the same moment that he felt a sting in his back pockets. He glanced around, and there was his mother wielding her Chi Omega sorority pledge paddle. Again and again, with unerring accuracy.

Mike gets a rousing welcome from his Little League teammates after hitting a home run.

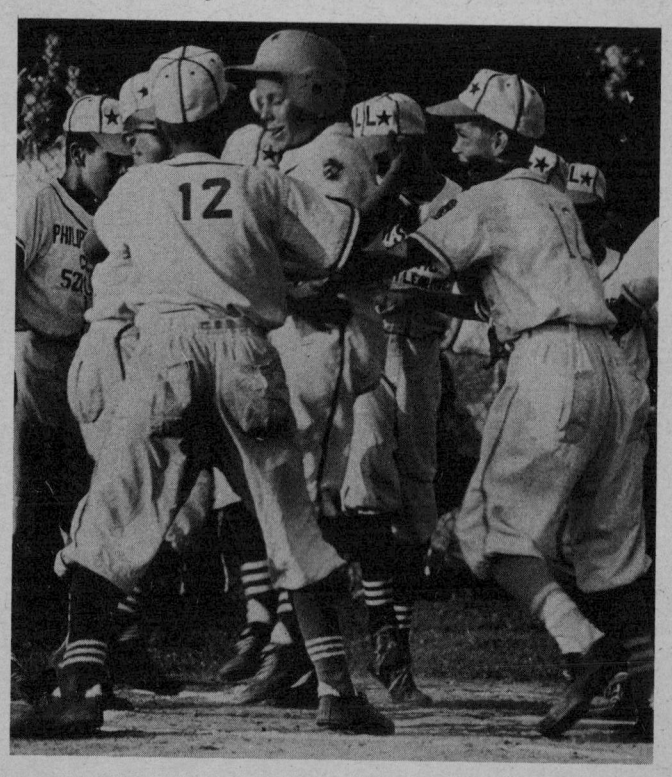

"I guess," his mother said, "now you'll be coming home when I call."

"Uh-huh," Mike said through his tears. And then he whispered, "Or else I'll remember to look behind the door."

Jack Schmidt had definite ideas about being a father. He wanted everyone home for dinner. It was a time for recapping the events of the day, being together as a family, making plans, solving problems.

Jack Schmidt did not believe in spoiling his kids. He felt that sports served a useful purpose, burning off energy, leaving a youngster weary enough to want to crawl into bed at nine o'clock, safe from trouble brewing in the streets.

It wasn't long before Mike had a summer job at Jack's Drive-In. He was paid 50 cents an hour to keep the place tidy. His equipment was a broom and a dustpan.

The following year he worked as a locker boy at his grandfather's pool, for the same pay. Pool customers would summon him to open their lockers. To make sure no one opened up someone else's locker, Mike would first ask the man for the color of his shirt and pants. Then he'd open the locker and peek inside, to make sure he'd opened the right one.

As the years went on, Mike continued to

hold a variety of summer jobs. He moved up from sweeper to counterman at the drive-in restaurant.

One year Mike worked behind a drive-in window, taking orders for "Swanky Franks" and chocolate shakes. Ice cream was five cents a dip in those days.

Another year he got to run the soda fountain, scooping baseball-sized blobs of ice cream from a rainbow row of containers, setting four milkshake containers humming at once, raising foam on sodas, king of a delicious territory.

The pay scale was the same at the pool, but Mike hungered for the most glamorous job of all, lifeguard. And one summer, having passed all the lifesaving courses with flying colors, he got the job.

Summer jobs were a way to earn extra money. What Mike loved most was playing football, baseball, and basketball. He dreamed of one day becoming a professional athlete in one of those sports.

At Fairview High School, Mike was an average baseball player—a switch-hitting shortstop known for his defensive skills.

In football Mike made the freshman team and then the varsity as a safety, the only sophomore on the squad.

In the third quarter of a game against

Colonel White High, Mike drifted back to field a punt. He was wearing high-top shoes and he started left, then twisted, trying to evade a tackler. The cleats on his left shoe stuck in the ground.

He crumpled to the field, then limped to the sidelines. By the time he got there, his left knee was so swollen they had to slice his football pants open with a knife.

Surgeons operated the next morning at Good Samaritan Hospital, repairing some of the torn ligaments with staples.

Before the knee could heal completely, Mike was playing basketball, his knee taped for protection. He was on a robotlike schedule of school, practice, dinner, homework, bedtime.

The following autumn Mike was eager to try football again. He brought the subject up timidly at the dinner table.

"I'm not sure it's a wise thing to do," his mother said.

"If that's what he wants to do, we can't hold him back," replied his father.

Three games into the season, Mike got to start at quarterback. He had been playing regularly on defense all along.

Against Belmont High, Mike covered the wide receiver. The pass was overthrown and Mike lunged for it, snaring it over his left

After knee surgery, Mike (32) didn't waste any time getting back into action—with the Fairview basketball team.

shoulder. He turned, feinting to shrug off the receiver. This time he heard something tear in his right knee.

He continued to play. But in September of his senior year surgeons again had to repair the damage. His football career was over and his baseball dreams were in danger, too, now that he had surgical scars on both knees.

3

A Switch in Time

Mike Schmidt's damaged knees discouraged most college recruiters. The mail brought feelers from small schools such as Muskegon, DePauw, and Defiance. Marietta was interested in offering financial aid if Mike would compete in three sports.

He started to abandon those visions of playing pro ball. But what would he do with the rest of his life?

Of all Mike's classes at Fairview High, only drafting excited him. He liked the challenge of duplicating blueprints, of drawing machine parts to make them look three-dimensional. He took pride in the leather case that contained his T-square, compass, and protractor. He began to consider a career in architecture.

Dr. Dave Reese, chairman of the Mid-American Conference, was a friend of Mike's grandfather. He knew the boy could play baseball, and he mentioned Mike's name to Bob Wren, the baseball coach at Ohio University.

Wren was recruiting Ron Neff, a strong-armed all-state catcher who played with Mike at Fairview High. Neff invited Mike to come along on a visit to the Ohio U. campus in Athens.

Wren had no scholarship aid to offer Mike, but the school had an excellent architecture department, the campus was pretty, and the students seemed friendly. Mike graduated high school in June 1967 and enrolled at Ohio U., a decision that would shape his life.

This is Mike's high school graduation photo.

Halfway through his first semester Mike got involved in a pickup basketball game on an outdoor court near the gym. Soon he was chipping the rust away from moves he hadn't made in years.

"You trying out for the freshman team?" he was asked.

"I guess I will," Mike said blandly.

He made the team and was soon starting at guard. That pleased him. But the other four starters were all on full scholarships, and that baffled him.

College basketball was a whole new world for Mike, crammed with calisthenics and rigorous conditioning drills. One drill called for side-straddle hops back and forth over a knee-high bench. You were supposed to do it for 60 seconds, but Mike would collapse, gasping, after 30 seconds.

The coaches sighed. But then the scrimmages started and the walk-on nonscholarship guard would pass and shoot so impressively that they'd forget about the bench drill.

But then one day Mike's world crumbled. An insurance examiner studied Mike's medical history and decided that he was too great a risk. So the coaches told Mike they had no choice but to drop him from the team. He turned in his uniform and fled to his dorm room, where he sobbed for hours.

The next day determination replaced disappointment. Mike knew that he might be barred from baseball, too, if he didn't rebuild those gimpy knees. So he reported to trainer Larry Starr, and they worked out a lifting program.

At first Mike could barely raise 20-pound weights strapped to each ankle. By the time the fall semester ended, he was lifting 100 pounds with each leg. But Mike had more work ahead of him if he wanted to make it in baseball.

Growing up, Mike had always flinched at curveballs, lurching out of the way, feeling embarrassed when they spun over the plate for strikes.

One day, when Mike was still in high school, Buddy Bloebaum, a scout for the California Angels, suggested that he switch-hit. He handed Mike a weighted bat, described a set of exercises, and talked proudly about a nephew he had taught to hit from either side of the plate. The nephew's name was Pete Rose.

So in Mike's sophomore year in high school he had started switch-hitting. He batted left-handed most of the time, because 90 percent of the pitchers he faced were right-handers.

Switch-hitting at Ohio, he struggled through

a .260 season as a freshman. And then Rich McKinney, the starting shortstop, was drafted by the Chicago White Sox.

By that time, Wren had wrangled a one-third scholarship for Schmidt. In the autumn of 1968 he took the youngster aside. "You've got a much better swing from the right side," Wren said. "I'd like you to give up switch-hitting and concentrate on hitting right-handed."

"I don't know, Coach," Mike said. "I'm liable to strike out a whole lot that way, bailing out when they throw me a curve."

"Stick with it and I'll stick with you," Wren responded. "Don't worry about the strikeouts. You've got a chance to be my regular shortstop."

That winter Mike hit hundreds of baseballs off a batting tee in the fieldhouse, using a weighted bat and swinging right-handed. Blisters formed, cracked, hardened. His hands got tougher, his swing smoother.

The next season Schmidt was Ohio's regular shortstop. He began hitting awesome drives in batting practice, rattling baseballs off Grover Center, the fieldhouse beyond the left-center field fence.

"Mike," Wren said, standing behind the batting cage, "I've seen big-league games, and

Shortstop Mike is the middleman in a double play against John Marshall University.

they don't hit them any farther there."

Schmidt blushed and then sent another long drive banging off the Grover Center bricks.

Each year Mike's batting average improved. He hit .310 as a sophomore and .313 as a junior, when he was named to the All-America team.

In his junior year Ohio qualified for the College World Series, a David in a field of Goliaths. Mike was wide-eyed at the prospect of going against teams that played 65 games a season in warmer climates, while his team was lucky to squeeze in 27 in the chilly Midwest.

Ohio's first-round opponent turned out to be Southern Cal, the nation's number 1 team, a squad that included a huge first baseman named Dave Kingman. Ohio won that game, 6–1, but lost to Florida State and Texas to wind up fifth in the tournament.

Disappointed as Mike and his teammates were, they had nothing to be ashamed of. They had made it to the College World Series.

4

Around the Horn

Tony Lucadello was a big-league scout who always wore a tie, even at a Little League game on some dusty field on the outskirts of town. He thought it added dignity to the job.

Wearing a tie wasn't the only thing that set Lucadello apart from the other scouts, with their stopwatches, clipboards, and notebooks. Lucadello didn't like to mingle with the others, swapping truths, half-truths, and lies in the rickety stands behind home plate.

Lucadello scouted Ohio, Kentucky, Indiana, and Michigan for the Philadelphia Phillies. He told people he wanted to be known as the best scout in baseball, to work for a pennant-winning team, and to someday be the highest-paid scout in the game. He told them little else.

"I don't like to let the other guys know who I'm looking at," Lucadello told a friend. "Sometimes I'll scout from behind a tree. And I don't spend a lot of time talking to the kids I'm scouting. The coaches resent it, and sometimes it messes the kids up."

You couldn't argue with Lucadello's success. He had signed Ferguson Jenkins, Alex Johnson, Larry Hisle, and Mike Marshall, all of whom became major leaguers.

Lucadello didn't talk to Mike Schmidt when he began scouting him as a sophomore in high school on the recommendation of a "bird dog" (an area scout).

He classified Mike as a "follow" (a prospect worth following), impressed by his aggressiveness but concerned about his inability to hit a curveball.

Lucadello followed Mike's career at Ohio and recommended him to Paul Owens, the Phillies' farm director. Owens made a trip to Athens to watch the prospect play, and the trip came perilously close to being a washout.

A Friday game with Bowling Green was rained out and rescheduled as part of a Saturday doubleheader. Owens had a plane to catch that afternoon, and he looked at the thick gray clouds warily.

Doug Bair was the starting pitcher for Bowling Green. Mike hit a mammoth homer off him that caromed off Grover Center. Lucadello sat there, grinning. But he kept glancing at his watch, worried that Owens might miss that plane.

"Don't worry," Owens said. "I wanna see this kid hit some more."

Mike hit some more. He also scurried from first to third on a routine single. And he went deep in the hole at shortstop to throw out a runner on a splendid play. He had done it all—run, thrown, and hit with power.

Owens, impressed with Schmidt's upper-body strength and his strong arm, turned to Lucadello and said, "That looks like our third baseman." And then he hurried off to catch his plane.

Mike finished his senior season with a .330 average, 10 homers, 13 doubles, and 45 runs scored. And he was again named to the All-America team. As his slugging increased, so did his confidence.

One evening, sitting in his dormitory with roommate Ron Morrison, Mike glanced up at wall posters of big-league pitchers Bob Gibson and Tom Seaver.

"One day," Mike said, "I'm going to hit a home run off those guys."

Shortly after Mike graduated, the 1972 free-agent draft took place. This is when the major-league clubs get to choose the eligible high school and college players. The Phillies gambled that other teams would pass on Mike as a first-round pick because of his battered knees. They chose Roy Thomas, a pitcher from Lompoc, California.

And then in the second round they chose Schmidt. He was the first college player selected in the draft.

The next day Lucadello showed up at the Schmidt home on Pinecrest Drive. He left his typewriter in the trunk of his car, another habit he'd developed through the years. He didn't want to appear too anxious. There would be time to lug in the typewriter to fill in the spaces on the contract once they had agreed to terms.

Lucadello sat on the sofa. Jack Schmidt was in an easy chair across the living room. Mike perched on a footstool, hyper as a sparrow. The air was charged with tension as the adults made small talk about the weather and the pennant races.

Finally Lucadello got around to talking about money. The Phillies were offering Mike $25,000 to sign, plus $2,500 each time he advanced a classification in the minor leagues, from A to AA, from AA to AAA.

Mike turned eagerly to his dad, who looked as if he'd been hit in the shins with a two-by-four. Jack Schmidt simply shook his head from side to side. He had been thinking in terms of $50,000 bonuses in the light of the six-figure contracts handed to such college players as Reggie Jackson and Rick Monday.

Lucadello returned to his room at the Holiday Inn in North Dayton and telephoned Owens. He glumly reported on the contract talks and suggested that they offer Schmidt $32,500 with the same $2,500 bonuses. Owens agreed.

The next day the Schmidts met with Lucadello again, this time in Lucadello's motel room.

"The place to make money is in the big leagues," Lucadello said. "We'll give Mike $32,500 and we'll bring him into Philadelphia so he can meet the players on the big club before we send him out."

Mike's eyes had a Christmas-morning glow to them now. Imagine traveling to Philadelphia, shaking hands with big-league players. He glanced at his father again. This time Jack Schmidt was nodding his head up and down. The deal was made.

The next morning Mike galloped to the White-Allen car lot. He swaggered to the Corvette section and pointed to a banana-colored Corvette, barely glancing at the $10,000 price tag.

"Are you sure that's the car you want?" the salesman asked.

"Mister," Mike said, "I've dreamed about a car like that for years. And now I can afford it."

The next day Mike and his dad were on a plane to Philadelphia. Frank Lucchesi was the Phillies' manager, a swarthy, friendly little man in charge of rebuilding a sorry ballclub. The Schmidts got to town on a Wednesday and were ushered into the clubhouse.

Mike blinked in disbelief. The manager had an office of his own, with a desk and a swivel chair. Each player had his own dressing cubicle. There was carpeting on the floor and beer in the cooler.

The clubhouse man was Kenny Bush, who had worked his way up the ladder from batboy to assistant clubhouse man to equipment man. Bush had a big heart but he also had the shortest fuse in baseball. He tossed a uniform at the newcomer.

Mike tugged on the white sanitary socks and

then the bright red outer socks. The stirrups were low and would show only a small wedge of white over his shoetops. Mike glanced around and saw guys wearing their stirrups high because it gave their legs a sleek, racehorse look.

Then he slipped into the pants. They were loose and rumpled. Mike slumped in his chair. He had always prided himself on his appearance. In the past his mother had altered his uniforms so that they fit snugly. And now he was going to go out onto a big-league ballfield dressed in baggy pants.

"Uh, Mr. Bush," Mike said politely, shuffling toward the clubhouse man. "I can't wear these socks, they're too low. And the pants, they're too baggy."

"Listen, rook," Bush said, the veins bulging in his neck, "this ain't Hollywood. You wear what I give you to wear, or you can go out there naked."

Mike finished dressing and walked down the ramp leading to the field, his heart pounding in his chest. Lucchesi was there, in the dugout, entertaining the media.

"C'mere, kid," Lucchesi said. "Let me take you around the horn." And he guided Mike out onto the field, toward first base.

"This," said Lucchesi, "is first base. This is where you'll get your signs."

The rest was a blur, moving to second, short, third. When the tour ended, Mike went back to shortstop, fielding groundballs alongside shortstop Larry Bowa, who seemed almost as irritable as the clubhouse man.

Then came batting practice. Mike took his swings in a group that included Byron Browne, Ron Stone, and Oscar Gamble, all bit players on a floundering Phillies team.

Despite his sweaty palms, Mike hit three balls into the seats in left field. And then he returned to the clubhouse, showered, and watched the game from a box seat.

The next day was an open date on the schedule. The U.S. Open golf tournament was being played in Merion, near Philadelphia, and the sports pages were crammed with golf stories. The Phillies had an exhibition game scheduled that night in Reading, Pennsylvania, against their Class AA farm.

"Bowa's got the measles or something," Lucchesi told Mike that afternoon. "You're gonna play shortstop for us."

While Mike rode the team bus to Reading, Owens drove the 60 miles to the ballpark with Jack Schmidt as a passenger.

"How do you think your kid will do?" Owens asked in his raspy, blunt manner.

"I think he may not hit much for average,"

Schmidt answered, "but I also think he'll hit a lot of homers."

The visitors' clubhouse in Reading was a cramped, airless room, but it seemed like a palace to Mike. He had a newer uniform to wear, and for the first time in his life he slipped into baseball shoes that weren't black. He tied the laces on his red Pumas and danced out of the clubhouse.

That night he played shortstop for a big-league team. And in the eighth inning he slammed a Mike Fremuth fastball over the fence in left field for a game-winning homer.

Mike rounded third, his eyes as wide as Little Orphan Annie's, almost hopping with joy. As he got to the plate Reading catcher Bob Boone said, "Nice hitting, Mike."

5

Minor Leagues, Major Problems

"Listen, kid," farm director Paul Owens said, "you're gonna finish out the year in Reading. That's a tough Double-A league. Lots of experienced pitchers. You'll probably see a lot of sliders and you probably won't hit too much, but you'll get your feet wet."

Mike Schmidt listened to the ominous forecast and then went out and fulfilled it. He hit .211, struck out 66 times, and made almost as many gloomy telephone calls home.

Each call ended with the same bit of advice from his father: "Keep 'er going, Mike."

His grandparents came to visit and found Mike sharing a cluttered room with pitcher Pat Bayless at a shabby downtown hotel. The room was dark and musty.

"How about letting us move you out of here," his grandfather said. "Let me get you a room at the motel near the ballpark. It's cleaner and you can room by yourself."

Mike's move to the Reading Motor Inn made his life more bearable for the rest of the season. Mike and the other players, including Bob Boone and Andre Thornton, checked the National League standings each day. They knew that the Phillies were a talent-poor ballclub and that any good young player in the farm system would have a chance to advance quickly.

When the season ended and the Phillies front-office staff met to discuss the minor leaguers, Granny Hamner, a member of the Phillies' 1950 pennant-winning Whiz Kids team, raved about Schmidt. Hamner, a roving instructor in the farm system, emphasized the eight homers Mike had hit that first year and minimized the strikeouts.

Andy Seminick, a catcher on that 1950 team, was going to manage Eugene (a Triple-A team—the highest minor-league classification) the following year. He asked to have Schmidt promoted to his club.

For half the 1972 season Mike did little to reward Seminick's confidence. He was playing third base and hitting .220. Second baseman John Vukovich was also struggling, and

Seminick summoned the two young players to his office. They wondered if they were going to be sent down.

"I'm going to switch you," Seminick told them. "John, you play third. And Mike, you're gonna move to second."

Startled by the move, but happy to be staying with the winning club in Eugene, Mike moved to the right side of the diamond. He worked at making the double-play pivot from a different angle and covering first on bunt plays. His mind crammed with fielding lessons, he had no time to worry about his hitting.

Before the season ended, he had boosted his batting average to .291 and was picked as the All-League second baseman.

The Eugene club prospered and qualified for the playoffs against an Albuquerque team that included such future major leaguers as Davey Lopes and Steve Yeager. And then, in a game in Hawaii, Vukovich fielded a groundball and flipped it to Schmidt, who was covering second. Mike got the force and then backed up to spin around and throw to first.

Instead, he went sprawling. His left knee had locked. They helped him off the field and sent him back to Eugene, where a doctor diagnosed the injury as torn cartilage.

Every September 1, major-league rosters are expanded from 25 to 40, and the brightest prospects are given a chance in the majors. Despite Mike's injury, the Phillies called him up, along with his Eugene teammates Bob Boone, Craig Robinson, and Mike Wallace. Boone, Robinson, and Wallace giddily pulled on big-league uniforms while Mike hobbled from whirlpool to dugout on crutches.

The Phillies sent him to West Park Hospital in Philadelphia, and Dr. John Royal Moore, an orthopedic surgeon, scheduled him for surgery.

Mike's mother flew in from Dayton to be with him. They prepped Mike for the operation, shaving the hair on his left leg, limiting his food intake, checking his medical history. That morning, Dr. Moore walked into Mike's hospital room at 6 a.m.

"You always so wide-awake?" Mike asked the surgeon, who was in his seventies.

"Son," Dr. Moore said, "I've been getting up at five in the morning for fifty years. Now, let me take another look at these x-rays."

Dr. Moore propped the x-rays against a transparent box and flicked on its light. He studied the gray sheets, his chin in his hand. Then he turned to the puzzled ballplayer.

"Come with me," he said, moving out into

the circular corridor. Schmidt, in his white hospital gown, followed.

"Let's jog," Dr. Moore said, and began to run through the corridor past the startled nurses. Schmidt tried to keep pace.

"All right," Dr. Moore said. "Now I want you to get down in a crouch, like a wide receiver, and then fire out."

Schmidt obeyed. He got creakily into a three-point stance, and on an imaginary "hike" command he bolted from the crouch to an upright position. He trotted down the hallway.

"I'm not cutting you," Dr. Moore said emphatically. "We're scrubbing the operation."

Dr. Moore was convinced that Mike's injury would heal without surgery, and he was right. By mid-September, Mike was well enough to play his first game in the major leagues—at third base.

Paul Owens had replaced Frank Lucchesi as the Phillies' manager. Owens wanted a closer look at the players and thought he could discover more about them in the clubhouse and dugout. His second day on the job he called a clubhouse meeting and slammed the doors shut.

"You guys got the team where it's at," he raged, staring at some of the veteran players. "And now I'm gonna play some of the younger guys. I want you pulling for 'em, rooting for 'em."

The rookies could feel the cold glares of the veterans. Larry Bowa had suffered through a dismal season. He looked at Mike and Craig Robinson as rivals for his job. But Owens stuck Mike, Craig, and Bob Boone in the lineup, and each of the three got his first big-league hit in the same game.

The Phillies won only 59 games that year, and Steve Carlton won 27 of those on his way to winning the Cy Young Award as the league's finest pitcher.

Carlton won his twenty-seventh game in Wrigley Field against the Cubs, with Mike playing third base. Ferguson Jenkins, a crafty veteran, pitched for Chicago and struck out Mike three times.

"I take a pitch and it's right on the outside corner," Mike moaned afterward. "I swing at one and it's a foot outside. I couldn't hit Fergy with a boat oar."

"Welcome to the National League," muttered Bowa.

Mike hit .206, striking out 15 times in 34 at-bats. But he got his first big-league homer off Montreal's Balor Moore. The Phillies had seen enough to think that Mike Schmidt was their third baseman of the future.

That winter, in Caguas, Puerto Rico, Mike found out just how much faith they had in him. A teammate rushed to his room with the news that the Phillies had traded third baseman Don Money to Milwaukee in a deal that brought pitcher Jim Lonborg to Philadelphia. Mike was suddenly the prime candidate to play third base when the 1973 season opened.

Mike arrived in Clearwater, Florida, eager to prove that the Phillies had made the right decision. He winced when he saw that they had bought infielder Cesar Tovar as an insurance policy, should Mike fail.

The Phillies had hired a new manager, Danny Ozark, a solemn man with a face as sad as a basset hound's. Ozark had spent 30 years in the Dodgers' organization as a player, minor-league manager, and big-league coach. He was a surprise choice.

Mike went all out to impress his new boss. He had heard the whispers about being too cool, about never dirtying his uniform while playing third base. So on March 26, in an exhibition game against the Cincinnati Reds, when Tony Perez rapped a ball to Mike's right, he dove for it.

Backhanding the ball, Mike sprawled into foul territory, landing on his left shoulder. He lay there, writhing in pain, clutching his shoulder. And then he went limp. He had fainted from the pain.

Trainer Don Seger rushed out and brought Mike around, using smelling salts. And then, realizing that the third baseman had dislocated his shoulder, Seger grasped Mike's arm tightly and shoved it back in the socket.

"I've never been so scared in my life," Mike confessed on the way to the hospital.

"Don't worry," Seger reassured him. "You'll be good as new in five weeks."

Mike beat the timetable, healing in Florida while the squad went north to open the season. In less than a month he was ready to return to action.

In a game against the Cardinals, Mike got to face the legendary Bob Gibson, the same man whose poster had adorned Mike's dormitory room at Ohio U.

Gibson threw a fastball that was waist-high and farther out over the plate than Gibson wanted it to be. Schmidt uncocked his wrists and, with a ferocious swing, belted the ball into the left-field bleachers.

A prophecy had been fulfilled.

6

"Dutch"

Mike Schmidt frequently struck out during his rookie year. That was painful enough, but his teammates added to the agony with their mocking laughter.

When Mike walked past Willie Montanez, the first baseman would often bark, "Ahchoo, ahchoo." Montanez was pretending to sneeze, as though he had caught cold from Schmidt's pitiful swings and the draft they created. It was a cruel joke, part of the hazing that goes on in the clubhouses of mediocre teams.

Schmidt was depressed, his confidence shattered. He wondered if he really could play ball at the major-league level.

Danny Ozark made Schmidt a special project. His motives were sound, but his methods were clumsy.

Ozark summoned Schmidt into his office for almost daily talks. He called Mike "Dutch" because of his German ancestry. Soon Mike had the feeling that whenever Ozark used the nickname, he was also implying that Schmidt was dumb.

Mike was a struggling rookie and he knew that rookies did not talk back to managers. So he bit his lip and kept swinging from the heels.

Some people did recognize the potential in this strong young man. "You remind me of Henry Aaron, the way you swing the bat," Chicago Hall of Famer Ernie Banks told Mike after a game at Wrigley Field.

"You're the first great hitter I've seen with a complex mind," teammate Davey Johnson said to him on a bus ride to the ballpark.

But the criticism outweighed the praise, and Mike stumbled through the season, barely hitting his weight, which was a little over 200 pounds.

Mike tried to ease the pain by partying nearly every night.

"If I do good," he told friends, "I celebrate by partying. If I do bad, I forget it by partying. I'm young; I can handle it."

He was single, drawing a big-league paycheck, staying in first-class hotels. The night life left him weary and sometimes hung over. He would sleep most of the next day, sometimes waking just in time to head for the ballpark and another disappointing game. Only the days off offered some solace. He usually played golf at suburban Philadelphia courses.

One September morning Mike played at Gulph Mills Country Club with pitchers Steve Carlton and George Culver. Afterward, hungry and thirsty, they stopped at the Valley Forge Stouffer's for lunch. The room was called the Grog Shop and it was dimly lit and very quiet.

Through the September shadows, Mike spotted an attractive waitress. She seemed uneasy in her skimpy costume, a mini-skirt and wraparound blouse. She also seemed unimpressed by her celebrity customers.

Donna Wightman approached the table cheerfully and took the players' drink orders. At the bar the bartender leaned over and whispered, "That's Steve Carlton."

"Steve who?" she asked blandly. "Oh, you mean the baseball player who does the paint commercials on television?"

The bartender shrugged. The waitress was new. He had known she was interested in music and had sung with a band that toured the country, serving as a warm-up act for the Byrds. Now he also knew she had no real interest in baseball.

When the waitress returned to the table with the drinks, Mike asked her name. And then he asked her for her autograph. It was a corny approach, but it tickled her. She wrote her name and telephone number on a cocktail napkin.

Mike tucked it in his shirt pocket and promised to call. He did, that night. He asked her out for Thursday, but she had other plans. She finally agreed to attend a Phillies' game that Sunday as his guest.

"You're going out with a .200 hitter," her father joked. "I don't know if I approve."

The trip to Veterans Stadium was an adventure for Donna. First a trolley ride from her home in the suburb of Erdenheim, then a rattling trip on the Broad Street subway line to the ballpark.

After the game Mike took her to a movie and then to dinner at a restaurant in Cherry Hill. Cesar Tovar sent over a drink.

The drive back to Donna's home lasted 75 minutes, with Mike grumbling about the distance. But they'd had fun and Donna felt comfortable with this easygoing midwesterner. The good feeling was mutual and it brightened an otherwise disappointing season.

Entering the final week, Mike was batting .205 and playing irregularly. Then Tovar decided he'd had enough of Danny Ozark's scolding. Tovar refused to play anymore, so the Phillies' manager wrote Schmidt's name in the lineup for the final three games in St. Louis.

Pitchers Bob Gibson, Rick Wise, and Reggie Cleveland combined to keep Mike hitless in 10 at-bats. That plunged his average to a dismal .196, with 136 strikeouts, for the season.

Young players in the major leagues are often assigned to the winter baseball leagues on Caribbean islands to get further experience. When the season ended, Mike reported to Caguas, Puerto Rico, for winter ball.

The Caguas manager was Bobby Wine. He was a former Phillies shortstop who had become a coach with the big-league club. Having seen Ozark frequently ride Mike, Wine decided to back off and give Mike's natural talents a chance to emerge.

Caguas had an excellent team, with a roster that included Gary Carter, Larry Christenson, and Jim Essian. Mike showed up at the ballpark early, anxious to take extra batting practice.

"Mike," Wine told him, "when you hit the

ball, you sting it. You just strike out too often. When you're up with a man in scoring position, you don't have to drive it seven hundred feet. Just hit the ball to right-center or left-center. Make contact. Cut down on the strikeouts.

"Relax. You're a good player, a good hitter."

Mike responded to the new, softer approach. Being in love with Donna was a boost. He was maturing as a person as well as a ballplayer. Caguas won the league championship and advanced to the Latin American World Series.

In a game in Hermosilla, Mexico, with the wind blowing in his face, Schmidt decided to put Wine's advice to work. He walked to the plate almost nonchalantly, took his stance, and held the bat lightly in his hands.

The pitcher threw a fastball over the inside of the plate. Schmidt swung at it easily, gracefully. The ball rocketed off his bat, but the wind stifled it and the left fielder caught it near the fence.

Schmidt returned to the bench ecstatic, as happy as if he'd hit a homer. He turned to Wine and said, "Did you see that? I went up there ho-hum and the ball jumped off the bat.

"All these years I've thought you had to

swing hard to hit it far. Trying to hit it far by swinging hard, that's what created all my problems. Now I know you can swing easy and get the same results."

7

An All-Star Surprise

In the brief gap between the end of the winter league season and the start of the Latin American World Series, Mike took the biggest step of his life up to that point.

He married Donna Wightman in February 1974 at his parents' home in Dayton before three dozen family members and friends.

Mike was blissfully happy when he reported to spring training in Clearwater, Florida, with his pretty new bride and his relaxed new attitude. The mood lasted about 48 hours.

The first time he walked into the batting cage to hit against "Iron Mike," the mechanical pitching machine, manager Danny Ozark was there, waiting for him.

"I've been thinking about the way you uppercut the ball," Ozark said, "and I want you to try something different. I want you to hold the bat the way Nate Colbert [of San Diego] does. I want you to start with it level instead of holding it upright."

Mike was demoralized. He had just come off a fine season in winter baseball, where manager Bobby Wine had done nothing but encourage him. And now he was being pestered again, this time to change his basic batting stance.

"Look, Danny," Schmidt said, summoning up his courage. "I want to be left alone. Right now I'm a good hitter. I have a good stroke and I don't want to mess with it.

Newlyweds Donna and Mike Schmidt look forward to a new life and a new season at Clearwater, Florida, site of the Phillies' spring-training camp.

"I'm staying on the ball, not yanking away. I've learned to relax."

"Yo, Dutch," Ozark answered. "A .196 hitter can't be stubborn. Try it my way."

Schmidt scowled and gripped the bat, grinding the handle in his fists. He gestured to the man feeding baseballs into the pitching machine to get it started. And then he took this new, awkward stance, with the bat resting on his right shoulder, parallel to the ground.

The mechanical arm cocked and released a baseball. It was a blur to Mike's angry eyes. He swung feebly and missed. And then he turned and stalked out of the cage, his face flushed.

"I can't hit that way," he muttered, and walked away.

The next day Mike sought out Carroll (C.B.) Berringer, Ozark's bullpen coach. C.B. was a go-between linking the manager and players, a gentle man with an old-fashioned crewcut.

"C.B.," Mike said softly, "you've got to get Danny off my back. They can send me to Triple-A, send me to Toledo, but I'm gonna hit my way."

The message reached club officials. When they met to discuss training-camp developments that weekend, Mike Schmidt's name was high on the agenda. Dallas Green was the new farm director, replacing Paul Owens, who had moved up to general manager.

"What are we gonna do about Schmidt?" Green asked.

"Why not just back off him and let him play," said coach Bobby Wine. "The more hollering and screaming we do, the more confused he's gonna get."

Ozark agreed to give it a try. He cut back on his lectures, stifled the temptation to tinker with Mike's stance and swing, kept silent when Mike botched routine plays at third base, and applauded the sensational plays he did make.

In 1973 Ozark had benched Mike against some of the tougher right-handers in the league. When Mike stayed mired in a slump, Ozark dropped him to eighth in the batting order, a spot usually reserved for scrawny guys, not 200-pounders capable of belting the ball 450 feet.

In the spring of 1974, determined to learn from his mistakes, Mike kept a diary in a black-and-white composition book.

"First game of the spring," he wrote on March 9. "Winter Haven. Started at third. Hit eighth. Given the green light on the basepaths. Hey, they finally know I can run a little. Hit a screwball off Bob Lee for a single. Singled off Rick Wise on a 2-2 curve ball."

Mike was learning to keep a tight rein on his emotions. When Ozark moved him up to the third spot in the order, he wrote, "Big deal. Uh-huh, the manager is showing some confidence in me."

A teammate glanced at the diary one day and then riffled through the pages, searching for a list of Mike's goals. Didn't he aim for 100 runs batted in, 100 runs, 100 walks?

"Nah," Mike told the guy. "I don't write goals down. I see some guys write their goals in their helmets and look at them every time at bat and that's okay if that makes them want it more. I can remember mine when I'm concentrating at bat. Besides, how do I know what I can achieve?"

He really didn't know. People always spoke of his potential in awed tones. It took Dave Cash to make Mike believe in himself. Cash was a scrappy second baseman the Phillies had picked up from the Pirates in a trade. When he wasn't grinding himself into shape in spring training, he was busy handicapping the greyhound dog races at nearby St. Petersburg.

One day Cash tipped his teammates on a dog he had been watching for weeks. The next morning, as the players lined up for calisthenics, Larry Bowa whispered to Cash, "Did he win?"

And Cash yelped, loud enough to be heard in downtown Clearwater, "Yes, he did."

A rallying cry for that young Phillies' team emerged from that dialogue. Can we win? they wondered. And Cash kept answering loud and clear, "Yes, we can."

Cash set to work restoring Mike Schmidt's shattered confidence. Cash talked softly about drives he had seen Mike hit in games against the Pirates. He stressed the remarkable fielding plays Mike had made.

"You know," Schmidt confided, "you're the first guy to ever pat me on the back, tell me how good I can be. Before you came along, all I heard was negative stuff. You really think I can drive in a hundred runs?"

"Yes, you can," Cash answered softly.

Mike began to believe in Cash's sermons on confidence. And on June 10, in Houston's Astrodome, Mike made headlines with an awesome drive that would change the look of the indoor arena.

Mike thundered into that game with a total of six homers and 18 RBI's in his last nine games and a .529 average for the month.

Claude Osteen was pitching for Houston. Mike came to bat with Larry Bowa and Dave Cash on base. Osteen threw a good pitch, low and away.

Mike's hips churned; the thick part of the bat met the ball and sent it rocketing toward the distant bleachers and the huge American-flag backdrop.

"Homer," Osteen muttered to himself, and turned to watch it.

"That's headed for the flag," Mike thought, and started toward first base in his home-run trot.

Then, incredibly, the baseball plopped to the ground in short centerfield. Greg Gross, the Houston right fielder, hustled toward it. He picked it up as Bowa belatedly dashed for third and Cash for second.

The ball had hit a loudspeaker hanging from the ceiling, 117 feet above the ground, and had rebounded onto the playing field. Instead of a memorable three-run homer, Mike had to settle for one of the mightiest singles in baseball history.

Osteen stood there, stunned. He shuddered, relieved that Schmidt had not hit the ball back through the middle of the diamond with that much force.

And then the pitcher stared up at the speaker, located halfway between second base and the centerfield wall, and wondered how far the ball might have gone if it hadn't crashed into the speaker.

Shaken, Osteen gave up a double to Bill Robinson, the next hitter. And when he finally got the side out, he walked into the dugout and sat next to Houston center fielder Cesar Cedeno.

"Cesar," Osteen said with a poker face, "how come you didn't catch that ball? You catch it before it hits the ground, he's out." Cedeno just grinned.

For the next few weeks engineers did surveys, trying to figure out how far the ball would have gone. One survey estimated the distance at 600 feet, based on the angle of flight when it crashed into the speaker.

No one had ever come close to breaking up the furniture before, but the Astrodome folks were taking no chances. The next day they raised the speaker 56 feet, tucking it closer to the ceiling and out of harm's way.

The homer-that-wasn't got Mike national publicity. He was on his way to a remarkable recovery from a wretched rookie season, and now more people were aware of him.

Because of his poor showing as a rookie, Mike's name was left off the All-Star Game ballot that is distributed to the public early in the season. Now the Phillies mounted a write-in campaign for their slugging third baseman.

An engineer at one Philadelphia radio station wrote Schmidt's name on 30,000 ballots, a practice that is allowed but not encouraged. The ballclub hired a helicopter and airlifted 100,000 votes to All-Star headquarters just in time to beat the election deadline.

With that kind of backing, Schmidt wound up with the most write-in votes in the history of All-Star voting. He finished second behind Ron Cey of Los Angeles, whose name was on the ballot. National League All-Star manager Yogi Berra of the Mets picked Schmidt for his squad.

"The guy is having a fantastic year," Berra explained. "And besides, I don't want to get shot next time I go to Philly."

Schmidt was one of four Phillies on the National League squad. The others were Steve Carlton, Dave Cash, and Larry Bowa. In the game, played at San Diego, Mike went to bat twice and walked both times.

The sportswriters kept needling Ozark for not having played Schmidt more often. "That may have been a mistake," Ozark admitted. "I just didn't want him to be intimidated by the tougher right-handed pitchers. We were trying to protect him."

Schmidt had an explanation for his dramatic turnaround. "The biggest difference has to be that I'm getting more relaxed. I wanted to relax last season, but I couldn't. I was tight as a drum.

"This year, when I go to the plate, I'd say seventy to eighty percent of the time I'm at ease, just looking to hit the ball hard somewhere. When you come up to the plate that way, your natural instincts take over.

"This year I don't have an 'out' pitch. There's no good way to pitch me. High and tight, low and away, if I'm swinging good, I hit it. You can go ask the managers and pitchers around the league, and you'll find they don't have any idea how to get me out when I'm swinging good."

Relaxed, taking a controlled swing, Mike wound up hitting .282 and led the league with 36 homers and a slugging percentage of .546. He also led the league with 138 strikeouts, but nobody scolded him for that.

He made only five errors after the All-Star break and finished second in the voting for Gold Glove third baseman. He also stole 23 bases.

Mike took time out to give credit to Cash and his enthusiasm. "Before, it wasn't too much fun to come to the ballpark," Mike said. "Then Dave came along and the atmosphere went from animosity and jealousy to team talk."

He also praised the calming influence of his

Outstanding at third base, Mike reaches for a wide throw on an attempted pickoff against the Los Angeles Dodgers.

wife, Donna. "Last year," he said, "I was single, and I'd never go home right after a game. Sometimes I'd be out until all hours of the morning. Things are different now that I have a wife to go home to. I'm not concerned with anything now except baseball and loving my wife."

8

"Captain Cool"

Mike Schmidt kept a little plaque on the top shelf of his clubhouse locker. His mother had painted it. The message said, "Who Can Think and Hit at the Same Time?"

In 1975 Schmidt's average plummeted and his strikeout total mounted. People took sides in a raging debate that mocked the little plaque in his locker.

"Schmidt thinks too much," some critics yelped.

"Schmidt doesn't think enough," others hollered.

Danny Ozark crooked his finger in Mike's direction and summoned him for another chat. "Schmitty," Ozark said in fatherly tones, "if you were dumb you'd be better off. There have been a lot of great dumb ballplayers, some of them so dumb they couldn't even remember yesterday."

Mike remembered yesterday, and the day before. And the memories of his 138 strikeouts in 1974 still haunted him. The writers didn't let him forget in 1975. They couldn't understand how Schmidt could strike out that often and just walk back to the dugout and slide his bat into the bat rack. They nicknamed him Captain Cool and wondered if any fire blazed beneath his icy exterior.

Billy DeMars, the Phillies' batting coach, studied Mike. He saw his strength, his incredible hand-eye coordination. If all that talent could be channeled for long stretches, DeMars knew Mike Schmidt could do heroic things.

"Mike seems to have that nonchalant looseness," DeMars would tell people. "He looks like he's not pressing, but he is. He hits the ball great in batting practice because he's nice and easy and relaxed. But in the game he tightens up, trying to hit the ball hard. He looks like he's trying to hit it to Trenton, New Jersey."

One day DeMars approached Mike and said, "Why don't you yell or throw something?"

"What good would that do?" Schmidt replied. "The pitcher doesn't get me out. I get myself out. Nobody's got more natural talent than I do. One of these days I'll put it all together for a whole season."

During the gloomy 1975 season Ozark dropped Schmidt from third to sixth in the batting order. "And he'll stay there until he cuts down on his strikeouts," Ozark promised.

Schmidt agreed that he was striking out more than he should. "No one with good hand-eye coordination should strike out that much," he said. "That's what makes them so hard to take.

"Natural God-given ability at anything is a gift. I've always had it. I can pick up a golf club and swing it like you're supposed to. I can pick up a bowling ball and bowl like you should.

"If I had decided to be a pro tennis player, I could have been. I've never fired a gun but I know with my coordination I could become a marksman if I tried."

But the Phillies didn't want a decathlon man. All they wanted was to see Schmidt slash the number of strikeouts while keeping his hitting powerful.

Schmidt fulfilled half the bargain, leading the league in homers again, with 38. But he also continued to lead the league in strikeouts, with 180. And his batting average dropped to .249.

While experimenting with his batting stance, Mike decided to work on the area above his eyebrows too. He tried Transcendental Meditation that season to help him relax but abandoned it after a while. And he found that Alpha mind control was not the answer for him either.

In 1976 he repeated the same distressing pattern, hitting another league-leading 38 homers, but striking out a league-leading 149 times while hitting .262.

"You're trying your damnedest," Schmidt said. "You strike out and they boo you. I act like it doesn't bother me, like I don't hear anything the fans say, but the truth is I hear every word and it kills me.

"Our fans overreact both ways. When you're in a slump they're brutal, and when you're going good they make you come out of the dugout and tip your cap for every little thing. They're so passionate, it scares the hell out of me."

The fans were passionate and they could also be bitter. "It wasn't just the booing," Donna Schmidt said. "It's the cruel things they say. I remember when I was pregnant for the first time. Crying all the time.

"I was at the ballpark and this fan kept saying how ugly I was. The tears welled up in my eyes. I stayed away from the park for a long time after that."

Mike's strikeouts were baffling because he did have such great reflexes, because he was a natural all-around athlete. He proved that in the spring of 1976 when he won $13,500 in the televised *Superstars* competition in Florida.

Still, he came stumbling out of the starting gate when the 1976 season began. But before the season was two weeks old, Mike made headlines once again.

It happened on a wild, windy day at Wrigley Field in Chicago. Danny Ozark had dropped Schmidt back down to the sixth spot in the lineup and Mike was downcast.

Dick Allen, the Phillies' first baseman, sat down alongside Mike in the visitors' clubhouse. "Mike, you've got to relax," Allen said softly. "You've got to have some fun. Remember when you were a kid and you'd skip supper to play ball? You were having fun.

"Hey, with all the talent you've got, baseball ought to be fun. Enjoy it. Be a kid again."

His mind eased by Allen's advice, Mike decided it was time to try a new bat. He borrowed Tony Taylor's flame-treated Adirondack model. It was an inch shorter and an ounce lighter than his own bat.

As though he were making a backhanded stab in the infield, Mike shows his tennis skills in television's *Superstars* competition.

Terry Harmon, another Ohio U. graduate in the club, offered to lend Mike his T-shirt, a tattered blue one.

"Hey, it's got a lot of hits stored up in it," joked Harmon, who played sparingly.

The wind was blowing toward the bleachers, and the Cubs rampaged to a 12–1 lead. Mike singled in the fourth inning, a line drive too low for the wind to aid.

He homered off Rick Reuschel in the sixth and again in the eighth. In the ninth, with two men on, he came to bat against reliever Mike Garman. Pow! Another homer into the left-field seats.

The game went into extra innings with the score tied, 16–16. Then Mike came to bat in the tenth inning against Paul Reuschel (Rick's brother) with a man on. He was swinging Taylor's bat, wearing Harmon's T-shirt, and grinning with the memory of Allen's pregame advice.

Reuschel tried to sneak a fastball by him and Mike connected. The ball caught the wind current and soared majestically into the left-center bleachers. The small crowd of Cub rooters groaned. And then the groans turned to cheers as they realized they had witnessed a chunk of baseball history.

It was the first time in 82 years that a National Leaguer had hit four consecutive homers in one game.

"When I first came to Wrigley Field," Mike said afterward, "they bled me to death with breaking balls. I was pulling around, trying to pump the ball out of the park. Slowly but surely I realized I could hit 'em out with a normal swing."

The home-run explosion may have been

Mike hits his fourth home run in a row against the Chicago Cubs for a record.

Schmidt's way of showing the manager he was no sixth-place hitter. But he didn't knock his manager.

"Ozark has a job to do," Schmidt said, "and he can put people where he wants. If he wants to hit me third, I'll bat third. If he wants me sixth, I'll bat sixth. And if he wants me ninth, then I'll bat ninth."

Mike's home-run barrage lit the fuse on an explosive victory streak. The Phillies won 51 of their next 69 games, pulling away from the pack in the National League East. In late August they led the division by $15^1/_2$ games.

And then came the plunge, like a boulder toppling down a mountainside. The Phillies' lead dwindled to three games over the Pirates. Philadelphia had not seen a baseball championship flag raised since 1950. The fans were horrified, then bitter as they saw the title slipping away.

"A nightmare," Schmidt confessed. "The hate mail, the letters saying we were choking, the abuse. I'd be out there trying to catch a tough grounder, thinking that what I did would decide whether we'd be $2^1/_2$ in front the next day or $4^1/_2$. Blow this one, I'd think, and I'll need cops to guard my house."

Eventually the Phillies pulled out of their

tailspin and clinched the division title in Montreal. The clubhouse exploded in a frenzy of champagne-squirting and back-slapping. But Dick Allen was nowhere in sight. He and two other black players, Garry Maddox and Dave Cash, had gathered in an equipment room, away from the sloshing champagne. Mike Schmidt joined them there.

Allen turned to the others and said, "I'd like to say a prayer." All four players bowed their heads, oblivious to the uproar outside, while Allen delivered a prayer of thanks for having shared the season together.

The players then drifted back to the main clubhouse, got doused with champagne, hugged and embraced their teammates.

Later, relief pitcher Tug McGraw mentioned the "separate" clubhouse celebration at a team meeting. There was a danger that the episode might become a racial issue.

Mike did not make distinctions between black and white. "Growing up," he said, "the athletes I admired were Jim Brown, Frank Robinson, Oscar Robertson, Walt [Clyde] Frazier. Clyde—I wanted to play basketball the way he did, the moves, the grace.

"And then it happened that my best friends on the Phillies were black. I feel guys become friends because they have similar interests. And I've learned a lot from Garry and Dick.

"Tug brought it up, but it's dead now. It wasn't a good scene. But it's over."

Philadelphia was humming with the Bicentennial celebration when the Phillies hustled into the playoffs against Cincinnati. But the Reds had too much depth, too much experience, and they swept the series in three straight games.

During the 1976 season Mike hit 38 homers to again lead the league, had 107 runs batted in, and a .262 batting average. And that winter he signed a new six-year contract for $565,000 a year. For a brief time he was the highest-paid player in the game.

The Phillies roared back in 1977, determined to win the division title again, to atone for their poor playoff showing, and to play in the World Series.

In July, Schmidt was on one of his blazing streaks when the Phillies faced the woeful Mets, who had lost 12 of their previous 14 games.

The New York pitcher, Jackson Todd, hit Garry Maddox with a ball early in the game. And then he beaned Schmidt with an 0-2 pitch that left an ominous smudge on Mike's red batting helmet.

Mike took one tentative step toward Todd, but then flipped his bat aside and walked woozily toward first base. Catcher Tim McCarver approached Schmidt between innings, asking about retaliation.

"Nah," Mike said. "I don't think the guy was throwing at me. Let's just play baseball."

So Steve Carlton breezed to a 12–1 victory without knocking down any of the Mets.

"That's the way to go," teammate Davey Johnson told Schmidt afterward. "They do that, just spit on it and keep going."

A week later the Phillies were facing their bitter cross-state rivals, the Pirates. In the seventh inning Pittsburgh pitcher Bruce Kison nailed Schmidt in the ribs with a fastball.

"Next time," Mike yelled at Kison, "I'm coming after you."

"Why not now?" hollered Kison.

Mike accepted the challenge and rushed at Kison, bringing both teams out of their dugouts in a stampede.

Mike took a couple of awkward swings at the Pittsburgh pitcher the Phillies had nicknamed the Assassin. Then Pittsburgh catcher Ed Ott surprised Mike from behind with a fierce tackle. Somewhere in the milling mob, the ring finger of Mike's right hand was fractured.

Kison, who was fined $50 for prompting the scuffle, said, "I give Schmidt credit for coming out. Talk is cheap. He backed it up. He earned my respect. I kind of enjoyed the whole thing."

Kison could smile because the Pirates rallied from four runs down to beat the Phillies. Tug McGraw was ejected for hitting Willie Stargell in the eighth, and the Pirates went on to win the game, 8–7.

The fight seemed to spark the Pirates. They overcame another four-run deficit to win the next game, and then swept a doubleheader, 5–1 and 12–10.

Afterward, Schmidt was glum. "I did exactly what I didn't want to do," he said. "I was trying to avoid that kind of thing the past two weeks. Guys were throwing at me tight, hitting me. I was mad, but I kept my head.

"I was proud of myself. I got hit twice in the Mets series, but I hung in there. After a while it gets to be a question of manhood. I guess the fans and even my own teammates were wondering how long I'd keep taking it. You can take just so much, and then it's pow, let's go."

9

A Look in the Mirror

Living in a lovely home in New Jersey, earning $565,000 a year playing big-league baseball, signing autographs for strangers, driving a high-powered car, Mike Schmidt seemed to be fulfilling the great American dream. Yet he felt that something was missing from his life.

"I stood in front of the mirror one day and asked myself what had I done to deserve all of this success and wealth and good fortune," Mike said.

"It just dawned on me that someone upstairs was taking good care of me. I couldn't have done it myself. At that moment a spiritual awareness came into my life.

"It didn't come out of a tragedy or a need. No fireworks went off. But I decided I ought to put the credit somewhere. I became a believer in a supreme being.

"I had always been out for myself, for number one, willing to advance at the expense of others, do anything to get to the top, to the major leagues, to wealth."

During the winter of 1976–1977 Mike had enrolled in Bible study classes with pitcher Jim Kaat and the Philadelphia 76ers' general manager, Pat Williams.

Armed with spiritual strength, Mike explained that he prayed for the mental strength to concentrate and the emotional strength to accept what was happening around him.

"I think my faith has made me more tolerant, especially of all those people who sit there and boo me," he said. "And I ask God to bless me and all the players with an injury-free game."

Even with the best of intentions, however, Mike occasionally lost his temper, such as the time when he brawled with Bruce Kison. Because of the broken finger Mike suffered in that scuffle, he couldn't swing his bat properly for a long time.

The injury cost him any chance of leading the league in home runs for the fourth year in a row. He wound up regular-season play in 1977 with 38 homers (14 behind league leader

George Foster of Cincinnati). He also drove in 101 runs and upped his batting average to .274.

Mike led the club in runs scored (114), triples (11), and walks (104). He won his second straight Gold Glove for fielding excellence.

Philadelphia again won the Eastern Division title, and the Los Angeles Dodgers won in the west.

The Phillies opened the playoffs with a 7–5 victory in L.A., but the Dodgers scrambled back to win the second game, 7–1.

The series moved to Philadelphia for the third game, and the Phillies breezed into the ninth inning with a 5–3 lead.

Gene Garber got two routine outs as the crowd cheered loudly. And then Los Angeles sent 41-year-old Vic Davalillo up as a pinch-hitter.

Coach Billy DeMars hollered from the dugout, "Watch this guy . . . he can bunt."

Shortstop Larry Bowa echoed the same warning. "Be on your toes," he yelled at second baseman Ted Sizemore; "this guy can bunt."

Sure enough, Davalillo bunted and scurried down the line, beating the throw. DeMars stared in disbelief.

Los Angeles manager Tommy Lasorda then

sent his best pinch-hitter, Manny Mota, to the plate. Garber, throwing sidearm, got two quick strikes on Mota.

Pitching coach Ray Rippelmeyer yelled from the dugout, "Make him hit your pitch."

Garber threw a slider and Mota hit it, deep to left field. Left-fielder Greg Luzinski broke in on the ball and then backed up frantically.

The ball landed in Luzinski's glove as he thumped into the fence, then it popped out and hit the fence. Luzinski caught the rebound as Mota chugged into second.

For years afterward Phillies fans would debate the presence of Luzinski in left field at that crucial time in the playoff game. During the regular season, manager Danny Ozark had used Jerry Martin as a defensive replacement for Luzinski in the late innings.

After Luzinski caught the ball on the rebound, he turned and threw toward second, although he had no play on Mota. The ball hit a seam in the artificial turf and bounced crazily away from second baseman Sizemore.

First baseman Richie Hebner chased it down, but by the time he caught up with it, Davalillo had scored and Mota had hustled to third. The Phillies were now clinging to a 5–4 lead.

Swift Davey Lopes was the Dodgers' next

hitter. He rapped a sharp grounder at Schmidt. The ball came careening off the Astroturf, hitting Mike on his left arm. As the crowd gasped in surprise, the ball bounced directly to Bowa.

Bowa grabbed it and threw to first, a throw that seemed to trail blue sparks. Lopes sprinted toward first as the ball zipped across the diamond.

Ball and runner arrived at precisely the same moment. All eyes were riveted on first-base umpire Bruce Froemming. He threw his arms out, palms down, and yelled, "Safe."

Mota scored from third and the game was tied. Garber, trying to pick Lopes off first, threw the ball past Hebner, and Lopes scurried to second. Then Bill Russell singled up the middle. Lopes scored, and the Dodgers had a 6–5 lead.

Mike Garman squelched the Phillies in the bottom of the ninth, giving the Dodgers a 2–1 lead in the playoffs.

Disheartened, the Phillies sloshed through a 4–1 loss to Tommy John the next night in a game played in a steady downpour.

Schmidt had a woeful time in the playoffs, just one hit in 16 at-bats. There was some solace in the off-season when Mike was named winner of the Wanamaker Award, presented to the player or team reflecting the most credit on Philadelphia that year.

The award carries a $1,000 prize with it, and Mike donated that check to the Gibbsboro-Voorhees Little League.

"Their field's a mile away from my home," Mike explained. "I go by it every day on the way to the ballpark. I thought I'd do something for the community."

In spring training the following year, Danny Ozark surprised Schmidt with another award, naming him captain of the Phillies.

"It's really something to think the players on this ballclub respect me enough to prefer me for the job," he said, after the players gave him their overwhelming approval.

There was one dissenting voice raised. "This team won a hundred and one games the last two years," muttered outfielder Jay Johnstone, "so what do we need a captain for?"

"I don't think it's going to be any real big deal," Schmidt said. "I'm not going to have a big 'C' on my uniform. I'm not going to be any different as a person than I am right now.

"The team doesn't need a guy to dive into bases like Pete Rose to turn it on. I'll lead by what I do on the field. If it still appears that

I'm nonchalant out there, well, that's the way I am on the field."

A season that started with such promise soon dissolved into misery. Mike suffered a severe hamstring pull that kept him idle for three weeks. When he returned, his batting stroke was rusty and clumsy.

The fans jeered every strikeout, hooted at every error. "The fans are trying to stimulate Mike," suggested Ozark. "They figure maybe he'll get mad and hit better. I don't think they're saying he's no good. They're just trying to stimulate something."

Jim Kaat, one of Mike's closest friends on the team, said, "These people don't care what you did yesterday. It's just what you do today. Fans are like that everywhere, but in Philadelphia it seems exceptionally so. They're tough and they keep you on your toes."

Schmidt just shrugged those massive shoulders and accepted the jeering. "I've decided," he said, "that I deserve to be booed. There's no question about it.

"If I had a 'boo' sign in my back pocket I would pull it out and help them. I just want the people to know I would be booing myself.

"About all I can do is go out there and swing my way out of it and hope the cream will come to the top."

When the Phillies were squandering their division lead late that year, Schmidt, as captain, called a clubhouse meeting before a game against San Francisco.

"What we've got to do," he told his teammates, "is concentrate on nothing but scoring runs. Think about any way you can get to first, think about any way you can get to home plate. Get your minds on nothing else."

The message was brief but effective. The Phillies returned to the pennant race with renewed determination.

Afterward, Tim McCarver approached Schmidt. The veteran catcher had spent hours boosting Mike's confidence in his skills, reminding him that he was the best player in the game. And he had spent considerable time poking fun at Mike's modest reaction to his own fantastic fielding plays. This time McCarver came to compliment the third baseman for his clubhouse speech.

"Mike," McCarver said, "that was your finest hour as a professional."

Those weren't Schmidt's finest hours at the plate, however. Although the Phillies won the division title for the third year in a row, Mike ended the regular season with only 21 homers and a .251 batting average.

The Phillies faced the Dodgers again in the

playoffs. Los Angeles romped in the opener, 9–5. In the second game Tommy John blanked the Phillies, 4–0, pitching a four-hitter. The series moved to Los Angeles, where the Phillies waltzed to a 9–4 victory with Steve Carlton going the distance.

Now it was the fourth game of the three-out-of-five series and the teams were tied three-all at the end of nine innings. After the Phils failed to score in the top of the tenth, Tug McGraw gave up a walk to Ron Cey and, with two outs, Dodger Dusty Baker lined one to center. The always dependable Garry Maddox moved in for the catch. But the ball dropped out of his glove and Cey went to second. Bill Russell came to the plate. On McGraw's second pitch, a high slider, Russell sent a looping line drive to center. Maddox tried in vain to scoop up the ball as Cey charged home with the winning run.

The Dodgers were National League champs again, and the Phillies flew home empty-handed.

10

Getting Ready

The Phillies eagerly signed Pete Rose to a rich contract before the 1979 season. He'd become a free-agent, Cincinnati didn't want him anymore, and Pete turned down better offers to play for Philadelphia. He preferred being with an offensive club that had a good chance to win a pennant.

Rose brought his head-first slides and all-out enthusiasm with him. More than that, he showed a keen interest in Mike Schmidt. He pointed up Mike's strengths and kept track of Mike's statistics just as he kept track of his own.

Indeed, Mike's statistics were noteworthy as he blazed through the early part of the season. By July 10 he had 29 homers. People were

Pete Rose (left) became Mike's teammate in 1979 and inspired the Phillies slugger.

comparing Mike's home-run record with those of Babe Ruth and Roger Maris. Ruth had hit 60 in a 154-game season and Maris had walloped 61 in a 162-game season. At the rate he was going, Mike had a chance to match or even surpass their feats.

Mike's blistering pace brought out the superstition in him. He rode to the ballpark every day with Garry Maddox and insisted on following not just the same route, but the same routine. Every day they would stop at a corner grocery store on Route 561 in New Jersey. Mike would buy a lime soda and a copy of the Philadelphia *Daily News*.

On the way, he would drink the soda and read the newspaper. After a while people asked Maddox if he wasn't weary of the ritual.

"The man's carrying the ballclub. I'd be crazy to talk him out of it," Maddox said. "It's whatever makes you relax, whatever gets you in the right frame of mind, whatever it takes."

Halfway through the season, Mike made a major change in his stance. He moved deeper into the batter's box and farther away from the plate. Legendary Pittsburgh outfielder Roberto Clemente had hit that way, and Mike had always admired his slashing style.

Mike singled his first time up with the new stance, but when he got to first base he was wearing a home-run grin. He liked hitting that way. And soon after, in the All-Star Game, Schmidt had an opportunity to test his new stance against flame-throwing Nolan Ryan, whose fastball was often a buzz saw that churned bats into splinters when he jammed hitters. Mike got the fat part of the bat on an inside fastball and hammered it into left-center for a double.

Late in the season farm director Dallas Green replaced Danny Ozark as manager of the Phillies. Green was a marked contrast to Ozark. Green was loud, outspoken, and harsh in his public criticism of the players.

He immediately stirred up a hornets' nest when he said he would use the final month of the season to "find out who wanted to play."

Schmidt expected that it would be a big adjustment for him. Except for his brief trial under Paul Owens at the end of the 1972 season, Mike had never played for any other big-league manager.

But the change to Green had no immediate effect on Schmidt. He was in a batting groove and oblivious to distractions.

Mike didn't break the major-league home-run record in 1979, but he did finish the season with 45 homers, second to Dave Kingman of the Chicago Cubs. He also drove in a league-leading 115 runs and cut his strikeouts down to 115.

Despite Schmidt's slugging and Rose's .331 season, the Phillies wobbled home fourth in a year of many changes.

As impressive as Rose was on the field, he had been even more impressive in the clubhouse. Rose had been captain on a championship team in Cincinnati. He was a World Series veteran, a future Hall of Famer who cared deeply about the game of baseball and was willing to share his knowledge with teammates.

With Rose on hand, Mike felt awkward about being team captain. Under Danny Ozark, it had been a simple function. The captain took the lineup card to home plate before games and discussed the ground rules with the umpires, but Schmidt knew there could be more to the job than that.

When Green replaced Ozark, Mike walked into the manager's office to resign his captaincy. "You've got Pete Rose," Schmidt told Green. "To me, Pete exemplifies what a captain ought to be. Me, I'm a lot less outgoing."

"Let me think about it," Green said.

He thought about it during the winter, and when spring training rolled around for the 1980 season, the Phillies no longer had a captain.

"We don't have a captain," Green said, "because we don't need a captain. What can a captain do besides take the lineup card to home plate? With my open-door policy, I don't need a go-between. A player has every right to come in at any time and say, 'Skip, can I have a few minutes?' If you're gonna lay the authority figure on them or play God, you're gonna back some people off. I don't see the need for a captain on a veteran club, other than Pete Rose, and Pete doesn't want the responsibility."

The loudest sounds that spring came from Green's mouth. He wasn't going to let the players forget their dismal fourth-place finish of the year before.

Green had them sweating like a team with something to learn: long workouts stressing fundamentals—and always, that shrill voice.

"I don't know if Dallas's screaming is all that significant," Schmidt said. "What is significant is that we're working harder and we're getting more accomplished. We'll execute better. We won't give as many games away, but it won't be because we're afraid Dallas is gonna yell at us.

"I know it won't bother me if he screams at me because, more than likely, I'll deserve it. If I'm lackadaisical, he should jump me. It doesn't hurt to get kicked in the rear end once in a while. It might make me a better player. It sure won't make me any worse."

Along with the loud voice, some new rules were emerging from the manager's office—some of them serious, some frivolous.

Green wanted to set up a dress code for road trips. It was up to Schmidt, who prefers casual clothes, to help decide what sort of jeans would be acceptable.

One other significant rule change involved card games in the clubhouse. For years the Phillies had killed the time before games by playing cards.

"We played hearts, and then tonk," Schmidt said. "We played bridge. Sometimes we played right up until it was time for the regulars to take batting practice. The years we wound up in the playoffs, nobody complained."

Green limited the card playing. Once batting practice started at home games, the card playing was to cease. On the road, early arrivals could play, but as soon as the bulk of the team arrived, usually two hours before a game, the cards or dominoes would be put away.

Infield practice became a constant source of irritation between the manager and the players. In the past a veteran infielder had occasionally been permitted to coax a second-stringer into taking his place in the pregame drill. Green allowed that practice to continue, but required the veteran to donate $100 to the Philadelphia Child Guidance Clinic every time he skipped a drill.

Down through the years Schmidt had developed a pregame pattern that did not always include infield practice. He would arrive at the ballpark around three o'clock for a seven thirty ballgame.

"If I'm in a slump, I'll come out early," he explained. "I want some extra batting practice—either in the batting cage in the tunnel or on the field.

"Besides, I like to get to the ballpark early because I don't like to hurry doing anything. I want to take my time. If I need to get into the whirlpool to soak my muscles, I want to be able to do that.

"The Phillies have a guy videotape every game. If I'm not hitting well, I'll turn that videotape machine on and watch my times at bat."

The pitchers take batting practice around four thirty. At that time Mike goes out and fields fungoes hit by coaches Bobby Wine or Deron Johnson. Then it's back to the clubhouse, where Mike usually goes through his mail.

"Everybody who writes to me gets an autographed picture in return," Mike said. "I've got a secretary who sorts out the business mail for me. I don't have time to read every letter. Few players do."

When it's his turn to take batting practice, Mike works on the things he's having trouble with. "If I'm being pitched in a certain way and not reacting in the game to those pitches, I'll ask the guy who's throwing batting practice to throw me those pitches.

"If we haven't seen a left-hander in a while, I'll ask Hank King, who's left-handed, to throw to me. I like the system best when the first four guys in the batting order take batting practice together, then the next four.

"We'll take eight swings, and then when it's your turn again, six, then six more. Then three, two, one. A coach like Dave Bristol, he throws rapid-fire. Wine keeps up a steady pace. Some other guys are too wild."

Mike doesn't try to put on a show in batting practice; no need to hit the ball into the seats. Half of his swings are just reinforcing good habits. The first few are for loosening up.

"Some guys have contests, trying to hit the long ball," Schmidt said. "A guy like Ozzie Virgil, he might hit five hundred homers in batting practice.

"But if I'm going to face someone like Houston's Vern Ruhle, the worst thing I could do in batting practice is try to smoke an inside fastball out of the park. I'm not going to see an inside fastball from Ruhle all night."

When his batting practice is over, Schmidt returns to the clubhouse and peels off his uniform, towels off, and then slowly puts on a clean, dry uniform.

About half of the time he will return to the field to take infield practice. That's a ritual many fans enjoy, because they get to see the regulars throw the ball around the infield in graceful patterns.

"In spring training I'll take it every day," Schmidt said. "But as the season progresses I slack off. If we go into Wrigley Field, though, with its grass infield, I make sure I take it there, to get used to the hops. In other ballparks with grass, I'll check to see how high the grass is, what the edge of the grass looks like."

Before home games Mike runs sprints up and down the ramp that leads from the clubhouse to the field. Then he usually goes into Gus Hoefling's training room and does some stretching exercises.

"Some guys do their running on the field, but I can't do that," he said. "Too many people call my name, wanting autographs, wanting me to stand still for pictures. It's too distracting."

The mood inside the Philadelphia clubhouse has changed through the years. In the beginning veterans like Willie Montanez would needle Schmidt by pretending to sneeze when Mike walked past. Now most of the players call Schmidt "Schmitty," but occasionally someone will call him "the big power hitter from Dayton." The needling is gentler, warmer.

For a while Jay Johnstone was the clubhouse clown, stuffing socks in his uniform shirt during rain delays to do imitations of Babe Ruth.

"No matter how close your team is," Schmidt said, "there are two or three general groups. The regulars identify with each other. The extra men hang together. And the pitchers stick together.

"Tim McCarver was one of the best guys we had at practical jokes, at keeping things loose. And Ed Farmer isn't too bad. The day after a guy pitches, Farmer will hang a number over his locker. It's supposed to be how fast the radar gun clocked the guy's fastball."

11

Leap Year

Mike Schmidt strutted into the 1980 season, confident, ready to put together a banner year at age 30.

"You're gonna be the MVP, Herbie Lee," teammate Pete Rose kept telling him. Rose had given him that nickname simply "because he looks like a Herbie Lee."

The nickname was all in fun, but the prediction about winning the Most Valuable Player award was serious. Rose had a long and proud history of playing with MVP's. Get on base often enough, as Rose did, and someone in the lineup is going to accumulate impressive statistics for driving in runs.

Joe Morgan (twice), Johnny Bench, and George Foster had all benefited from Rose's presence at the top of Cincinnati's lineup and become MVP's.

When the Phillies signed Rose before the 1979 season, they were weary of stumbling through playoffs, so they'd gone for a man with playoff and World Series experience, hoping his confidence would rub off on his new teammates.

"I came over here, hit .331, got two hundred hits, and played every day, come hell or high water," Rose said. Even though the Phillies wobbled home fourth, Rose's enthusiasm and his pride had an impact.

He continued to praise Schmidt. "There are players who run faster, or hit for higher averages, steal more bases," Rose said, "but he does everything. He's the best player in the game."

Schmidt responded to Rose's encouragement in 1980. He was voted player of the month in May when he hit .305 with 12 homers and 29 RBI's.

He received the most votes of any National Leaguer in the All-Star balloting, but a pulled hamstring muscle kept him on the bench the night of the big game.

He hit two homers in one game five times, giving him a career total of 25 such games.

And he was on his way to his fifth Gold Glove award for fielding excellence.

September was a vivid mixture of joy and sorrow. Viola Schmidt, Mike's grandmother, died of cancer at the age of 75 on September 26, the eve of Mike's thirty-first birthday.

Mike had fond memories of the little woman with the strawberry-blonde hair who had pitched a Wiffle ball to him in the backyard. The same woman who followed his career, her ear glued to a radio that sputtered with static, cheering his big-league heroics in other cities.

"I've been thinking about her a lot lately," he said. "I'd like nothing better than to win the Most Valuable Player award for her. I had hoped she would hang on and see it happen. But even now it would mean a great deal to me to win it."

He went straight from the funeral in Dayton back to the heat of the pennant race. "My first day back, we were playing the Cubs," Mike recalled. "They brought in Dennis Lamp to pitch to me in the fifteenth, with the tying run on third. I popped up the first pitch.

"Garry Maddox was on the bench, not too happy with the manager, Dallas Green. But Dallas sent Garry up with two out and Garry got a base hit that tied the game and erased my out.

"Then Manny Trillo hit a ball up the middle to bring the winning run in. That took a load off my shoulders."

The dramatic extra-inning come-from-behind victory took a load off Green's shoulders too. The explosive manager had benched three of his regulars—Maddox, Greg Luzinski, and Bob Boone—in a move designed to shake up the team.

The next night rookie pitcher Marty Bystrom ran his record to a gaudy 5-0 as the Phillies pounded the Cubs, 14–2. Montreal, though, remained a half-game in front with a 5–2 victory over St. Louis.

Green stuck Maddox, Boone, and Luzinski back in the starting lineup the next day, but Maddox complained about an injured finger and was replaced by Del Unser.

Steve Carlton pitched a two-hitter and the Phillies won, 5–0. Meanwhile, Montreal blanked the Cards, 8–0.

The Expos were idle the next day, when the Phillies played their final home game of the season against the Cubs. Another rookie, Bob Walk, started for the Phillies. He gave up a run in the first inning, then pitched gallantly until the eighth.

Randy Martz faced Schmidt in the fourth, and Mike lashed a home run that rocketed over the center-field wall. It was Mike's forty-sixth of the year.

The Phillies picked up a pair of unearned runs in the eighth, and reliever Tug McGraw saved the victory for Walk. The Phillies were now dead even with Montreal, with three games against the Expos left on the schedule.

The Phillies had won 19 of their last 25 road games when they took the field at Montreal's Olympic Stadium.

Schmidt had crawled out of bed that morning coughing and wheezing with flu symptoms. He refused to take any antibiotics for fear of side effects that would leave him light-headed.

Pete Rose led off the game with a single to center, and Bake McBride doubled him to third. Then Mike lofted a fly ball to right, deep enough to allow Rose to score.

Dick Ruthven nursed that one-run lead through five innings, matching Scott Sanderson pitch for pitch.

In the top of the sixth, Schmidt faced Sanderson once again. The right-hander threw a fastball and Schmidt hammered it deep into the lower deck in left-center.

It was Mike's third home run in three days,

Mike slams his forty-sixth home run, the most he'd hit in one season.

and his eighth in 14 games.

Montreal got a run in the bottom of the sixth, but Sparky Lyle squelched that rally. And then Tug McGraw pitched the final two innings in impressive fashion. The Phillies' 2–1 victory put them one game up with two games left to play.

"Maybe it was better that I had the flu," Mike said afterward. "I didn't get all tensed up like I usually do for big games. I didn't try to do something super-human."

The next morning the Phillies woke to find rain lashing at their hotel windows. The weather forecast was grim, calling for an all-day rain. The game was scheduled for 2:15 to fit in with NBC television programing.

It was raining at game time, so the Phillies trudged back inside their clubhouse to wait. They waited and waited and waited, for more than three hours. The game finally began at 5:25.

After some weird baserunning blunders, the Phillies managed to squirm into a 3–2 lead in the top of the seventh. But Montreal got two runs in the bottom of the inning for a 4–3 edge.

The game rumbled into the ninth, with Woodie Fryman pitching for the Expos. Fryman walked Rose on four pitches. Bake

McBride bounced to Rod Scott, who tagged Rose. Schmidt topped a 3-2 pitch toward third and was out on a bang-bang play, but McBride made it to second.

Then Bob Boone ripped Fryman's 1-0 pitch into centerfield. McBride stumbled rounding third but scored the tying run.

McGraw pitched two harrowing innings as the teams remained deadlocked. In the top of the eleventh, Rose led off with his third single. McBride fouled out to Gary Carter. Now it was Schmidt's turn.

After falling behind, 2-0, reliever Stan Bahnsen decided to challenge Schmidt with a fastball. Schmidt was ready. He swung and the ball scorched through the soggy air, landing in the left-field seats for a two-run homer.

It was Schmidt's forty-eighth home run, a National League record for third basemen. Schmidt danced around the bases, and as he rounded third his teammates tumbled out of the dugout. As soon as he stomped on home plate, they swarmed all over him, hugging him and exchanging high-five handslaps.

Now it was up to McGraw to nail down the division title. Gary Carter popped to Rose. Warren Cromartie flied to left. And then McGraw pumped a called third strike past Larry Parrish.

McGraw leaped high, punching the air with his fists. The Phillies had won the title and the celebration had begun.

"This is very meaningful to me," Schmidt said in the noisy clubhouse. "Not many people thought we could come up here and take two from them in their own park. But we did it. I am deeply satisfied. Today, I made it happen.

"There's all the heart possible in this dressing room right now, but if we don't win the playoffs, people will call us the same old Phillies."

The Phillies had to sweat out a tight finish in the West before they even knew who their playoff opponent would be. Houston, having squandered a three-game lead with three to play, blitzed the Dodgers in a one-game playoff, 7–1.

"The whole team is looking at the playoffs differently this time," Schmidt said. "Oh, it's the same bunch of guys who have had a great deal of adversity in common. But this team has character. The way we're playing now, the team has proven to me it's ready to play the best teams in baseball."

The Phillies hadn't won a post-season game at home since 1915, when Grover Cleveland Alexander beat the Red Sox at Baker Bowl.

If history was against the Phillies, they had Steve Carlton going for them. And Carlton pitched seven gutsy innings before Green called on the magical McGraw to nail down a 3–1 triumph.

Houston got even the next night, grinding out a 7–4 victory in 10 innings.

The pitchers dominated the third game, which was scoreless through 10 innings. In the eleventh, little Joe Morgan of the Astros led off with a triple. Green ordered two intentional walks to fill the bases.

Then Dennis Walling hit a sacrifice fly on an 0-2 pitch to score pinch-runner Rafael Landestoy. Houston won, 1–0, taking a 2–1 edge in the best-of-five series.

The fourth game was filled with controversy. In the fourth inning Bake McBride and Manny Trillo singled off Houston's Vern Ruhle. With nobody out, Garry Maddox hit a soft liner back at Ruhle. Ruhle threw to first baseman Art Howe to double up Trillo, and then Howe ran over to tag second base (which McBride had deserted) for a seeming triple play.

The Philadelphia players swarmed out of the dugout, claiming that Ruhle had trapped the ball (caught it on a bounce). Plate umpire Doug Harvey, his vision obstructed when

Maddox broke from the plate, had ruled it a fair ball, but when he saw Ruhle fire the ball to first base, he asked his fellow umpires for an opinion and they said that Ruhle had caught the ball on a fly.

After 20 minutes of debate, however, Harvey disallowed the put-out at second, placing McBride back on second because it was the umpire's no-catch gesture that had caused McBride to leave second base in the first place.

Another disputed call went against the Phillies, and a Houston run was disallowed when the umpires ruled that the runner had left third too early on a sacrifice fly.

The score was tied, 3–3, after nine wild innings. In the tenth Pete Rose crashed into catcher Bruce Bochy to score the winning run, and Manny Trillo drove in an insurance run for a 5–3 triumph.

It was hard to imagine that the two teams could top those thrills and excitement, but that's just what they did in the fifth game.

Houston led, 5–2, after seven innings. Nolan Ryan, the Astros' great pitcher, was on the mound. But he was facing a team that wouldn't die.

Rose battled Ryan to a full count with the bases loaded, then walked to force in a run. Joe Sambito replaced Ryan, and pinch-hitter

Keith Moreland's force-out drove in another run, cutting the Astros' lead to 5–4.

Ken Forsch came in to pitch to Schmidt and struck him out. But pinch-hitter Del Unser singled to tie the game, and Manny Trillo tripled in two more runs for a 7–5 advantage.

Houston rallied to tie the game and send it into extra innings. Unser came through again, doubling to right. Trillo flied to center, but Garry Maddox doubled to put the Phillies in front again.

Dick Ruthven stormed through a 1-2-3 inning and the Phillies were National League champions. The ghosts of past playoffs had been buried.

After the game Schmidt brooded briefly about that strikeout in the eighth inning. "I felt terrible," he confessed. "But before I had my helmet back in the rack, Unser singled. And before I slid my bat in the bat rack, Trillo tripled. That's what this team is all about, one guy picking another guy up."

Before the World Series began, Rose talked quietly with Schmidt. "You're gonna have some fun now," Rose said. "This is the best time of your life. There'll be hundreds of writers around. Talk to 'em. Laugh with 'em. Joke with 'em. You relax, enjoy yourself, and pretty soon you'll be playing well."

The largest crowd in Veterans Stadium history—65,791—turned out for the opener against the American League champion Kansas City Royals. They cheered themselves hoarse as the Phillies rallied from four runs down to a 7–6 win.

The Phillies had to come from behind in the second game, trailing 4–2 in the eighth. Bob Boone worked Dan Quisenberry for a walk. Del Unser pinch-hit for Lonnie Smith and doubled to score Boone.

Rose grounded out, Unser taking third. And then Bake McBride tied the game with a single.

Schmidt doubled to right field and McBride sprinted home for a 5–4 lead. Mike alertly took third on the throw home and scored the fourth run of the inning as Keith Moreland singled to center. The Phillies won, 6–4.

Kansas City took the third game, 4–3, despite Schmidt's first post-season homer.

And then Kansas City tied the Series with a 5–3 victory. "We're right back to square one," Schmidt said. "I'm not worried about this team. We've had our backs against the wall most of the year and we've come through."

Schmidt came through in the fourth inning of a scoreless fifth game. Bake McBride was safe on an error, and then Schmidt blasted a

2-2 pitch over the center-field wall at the 410-foot sign.

However, the Phillies trailed, 3–2, going into the ninth inning. Kansas City manager Jim Frey warned third baseman George Brett to be alert for a Schmidt bunt, so Brett moved in about five steps from his normal position when Mike came to bat.

Schmidt lashed a hard shot at Brett that bounced off his glove for a single. Pinch-hitter Del Unser quickly tied the game with a double. Then Moreland sacrificed Unser to third, and Trillo rapped an infield hit off the glove of Royals' relief ace Dan Quisenberry for the go-ahead run.

McGraw squirmed through the ninth and the Phillies had a 4–3 victory and a 3–2 edge in the World Series.

In the third inning of the sixth game back at Veterans Stadium, Schmidt came to bat with the bases loaded. Rich Gale threw a fastball on the inside part of the plate and Schmidt lined it into right-center for a single. Bob Boone and Lonnie Smith scored on the play, and the Phillies led, 2–0.

"I just had to relax and put the ball in play," Schmidt said afterward. "It was the first pitch he threw me inside. I just inside-outed it."

The Phillies widened their lead to 4–0 in

the sixth inning. In the eighth, the Royals scored a run and Tug McGraw replaced Steve Carlton.

In the ninth, Kansas City loaded the bases with one out. Frank White lofted a foul near the Phillies' dugout. Bob Boone lunged for the ball, then watched as it squirted out of his glove. But Pete Rose was right there to grab it before it hit the ground.

That brought up Willie Wilson. McGraw got ahead 1-2 and then threw a screwball. Wilson swung and missed, and the Phillies were world champions.

The crowd went berserk but stayed in the stands because a corps of Philadelphia policemen, some with snarling police dogs, others on horseback, had surrounded the playing field.

That left the stage to the players, and they acted out their joy in the traditional mob scene near the pitcher's mound. This one was a little different, though.

On the way to the ballpark that day Schmidt had needled McGraw. "You're gonna be in there," he said. "And you're gonna get the last out.

"Well, you've had your picture in the paper too much. And the pitcher is always the guy the photographers snap. Last year it was Kent Tekulve with his arms raised. So this time you better wait for me. I'm gonna be in that picture."

McGraw struck out Wilson and began to pound his thigh with his glove, the way he always does in moments of joy. And then, from deep behind third base, came Mike Schmidt. He hurtled the final four feet, landing atop the swarm of players near the mound.

"I loved it," McGraw said afterward, soaked with champagne. "Here's a guy with a reputation of being so cool and unemotional, of never letting himself go."

No one questioned Schmidt's right to leap atop the mob. He had hit .381 in the World Series, with two home runs and seven RBI's. He was voted the Most Valuable Player in the Series.

12

Most Valuable Lessons

The World Series cheers were still ringing in his ears when Mike flew to Hilton Head, South Carolina, to play host at his annual golf tournament. He still felt that inner glow when he rushed to New York to receive the World Series MVP trophy and a $5,000 scholarship check, which he donated to Ohio University.

A teammate turned the sweet moment sour, however, telling a Philadelphia *Daily News* columnist that there were other, more worthy candidates for MVP honors. He suggested that Mike had been too streaky a hitter to earn National League MVP laurels.

Schmidt was deeply wounded by the story. The player then told him he had been misquoted. Even if Mike accepted the inaccuracy

Mike receives the 1980 World Series Most Valuable Player trophy from Baseball Commissioner Bowie Kuhn (left) as Phillies' manager Dallas Green enjoys the ceremony.

of the story, he still could not help wondering about its timing.

Two weeks after the Series ended, the Baseball Writers Association of America announced its MVP choice: Mike Schmidt—unanimously. It was only the second time in the history of the voting that a player had swept all the ballots.

At the Philadelphia sportswriters banquet that winter, where he was honored as the professional athlete of the year, Mike charmed the audience by saying, "Only in Philadelphia can you experience the thrill of victory one night, and the agony of reading about it the next day."

Mike Schmidt had come an incredibly long way from the baffled rookie who'd hit .196 to the unanimous MVP selection.

And when it came time to list the highlights of his career, Mike ignored all his dramatic homers to describe that single in the final game of the World Series.

"The game-winning hit in the final game of the Series—I guess you can't do anything better than that," Schmidt said.

"I'll stand behind what I've always felt about personal goals being less important than team goals, but that has to be the highest point of my athletic career, without question."

He obviously meant what he said. He ranked the single to the opposite field higher than his four home-run titles, higher than the four homers he belted that one afternoon in Chicago, higher than the four Gold Gloves or All-Star Game selections.

"Maybe against Houston in the playoffs," he said, "on one or two at-bats I tried to do too much. Tried to carry the club, break a game open. I wound up carrying the bat back to the dugout."

The city of Philadelphia honors Mike as Grand Marshal of its 1980 Thanksgiving Day parade.

No one accused him of thinking too much anymore. He had developed his new batting style on his own. Other hitters now came to him for advice.

"I went to that off-the-plate, deep-in-the-box stance because I was having trouble with pitches on the inside part of the plate," he explained. "Now I can hit that pitch consistently and I feel very comfortable.

"All the good hitters I've ever seen stride into the ball or into the plate. George Brett hits that way. Roberto Clemente hit that way."

Now no one kept track of Schmidt's late-inning homers with the bases empty or implied that he did not deliver in clutch situations.

"I'm not going to praise myself as a clutch hitter because I have failed in the clutch," he said humbly. "But at least now, in the clutch, I have a good chance of being successful."

Despite his October heroics, Schmidt still wore the tag of a streak hitter, prone to agonizing slumps.

"I'm never going to say, 'Hey, I know how to stop a slump,' or 'I know how to prevent going 0-for-15,'" he said. "But I feel I have a pretty good grip on my batting style, and a pretty good knowledge of how things go wrong when they go wrong, and a pretty good knowledge of why things are right when they go right."

And despite his emotional leap after the final out of the World Series, he was still Captain Cool.

"I want to convey to my teammates and to the opposition that I'm in control of myself," Schmidt explained. "I don't want anyone to think I am intimidated by anything that goes on out on the field, whether it is being done well or poorly.

"I always like to keep the opposition feeling I'm in control of myself, especially offensively. I feel that in order to succeed as a hitter, you have to have as much poise as you can possibly have while you're hitting.

"The same is true defensively. The more tension and pressure you put on yourself as a fielder, the more balls are apt to carom off your body and go too far away for you to field them.

"But if the ball takes a bad hop and hits a loose, relaxed, limp body, it's more apt to just drop straight down. Sometimes maybe I appear to be too cool on the outside. But there are times when I'm battling negative thoughts."

It seemed the only negative thoughts badgering Schmidt at the beginning of the 1981 season involved the threat of a players' strike. Shunting those gloomy thoughts aside, Schmidt ripped off a 13-game hitting streak in April and batted in 10 game-winning runs.

On Mother's Day in May, Mike had more cause for cheer. Little League baseball honored his parents, Lois and Jack Schmidt, as Little League Parents of the Year.

He was hitting .283 with 14 homers when the season screeched to a halt and the players went out on strike. The players wanted a looser form of free-agency, which would give them more freedom to change teams after they'd played six years in the major leagues.

During the strike Mike went to work at

With Mike looking on, Little League Commissioner Creighton Hale (left) congratulates Mr. and Mrs. Jack Schmidt as Little League Parents of the Year.

WCAU-TV in Philadelphia as its Sunday sports commentator. He wasted no time in stirring up a controversy.

His very first editorial involved the baseball strike. He said that the players had attempted to settle the dispute while the "owners went out and bought insurance."

Critics wondered how a high-salaried player could deliver an unbiased editorial commentary on the baseball strike.

"I was simply stating facts," Mike argued in his own defense. "I'm not a baseball player when I'm doing the news. I'm a newscaster. I really felt I wanted to give the public some meat in my debut.

"The strike is a hot issue. I didn't say anything that wasn't an exact fact. If an owner wants to come on as a guest or something and state exact facts, he's welcome."

Schmidt seemed nervous during his first sportscast. "I had a whole stomach full of butterflies," he admitted. When he got home late that night, Donna was already asleep, having taped the eleven o'clock newscast on their Betamax recorder.

So Mike celebrated his first night as a sportscaster alone, devouring a pint of fudge ripple ice cream.

When the season finally resumed after 49

days of idleness, Schmidt picked up his earlier pace. He was chosen National League player of the month in August, hitting .380 with 9 homers and 24 runs batted in.

His average zipped over the .300 mark on August 25 and remained there for the rest of the season. His final three at-bats were all three-run homers.

In that strange, strike-shortened season full of labor strife, Mike Schmidt led the league in homers with 31, in runs batted in with 91, and in walks with 73. He batted .316.

It was the fifth time he had led the major leagues in homers. Only Babe Ruth (11 times) and Ralph Kiner (7) had done it more often. (Ruth shared the home-run crown twice, Kiner three times.)

Mike made his sixth appearance on the All-Star roster, and this time he won the game with a two-run homer off relief wizard Rollie Fingers. He also won his sixth Gold Glove for fielding, setting a record for third basemen.

Seagram's selected him for its Seven Crowns of Sport award as "the most consistent and productive player in major-league baseball."

And then, like the cherry atop the sundae, came Mike Schmidt's second consecutive Most Valuable Player award. This time he was chosen first on 20 of the 24 ballots. He became the third National Leaguer to win back-to-back MVP trophies. The other two were Ernie Banks (1958–1959) and Joe Morgan (1975–1976).

Writers asked Schmidt if he had plans for joining Stan Musial and Roy Campanella as the only three-time winners in the National League's long history.

"I'm going out to improve," Mike answered.

This time there was no criticism from teammates or opponents, but Schmidt still seemed subdued.

"Nothing will ever top 1980," he explained. "I'll never have the inner feeling of satisfaction, or the inner glow, or the outer glow, that I had that year.

"Without question, my reason for the success I've enjoyed this year, last year, and the year before, first of all, I feel, has to do with my Christian foundation and the ability to take the pressure of having to succeed out of my game."

He had fulfilled Pete Rose's prediction by winning the MVP award again, and now he took time out to give credit to his outspoken teammate.

"Pete's constant badgering about how good I could be, and about how good he thought I was, boosted my confidence," Schmidt said.

"He set an example second to none. The enthusiasm he has for the game of baseball . . . that makes what I do fun."

Even though Paul Owens was faced with the problem of negotiating a new contract with his slugging third baseman, the general manager couldn't resist joining the chorus of praise for Schmidt.

"He's the best player in the big leagues," said Owens. "He makes plays no one else can make. The guy's like a ballet dancer sometimes.

"If we played 162 games this year instead of 107, he might have had 150 runs batted in. And his homers would have been in the 45 to 50 class. Add his .316 batting average and it's his greatest year."

By leading the division when the strike hit, the Phillies had clinched a spot in the post-season playoffs. The second half of the disrupted season turned out to be an awesome one for Schmidt.

"Maybe I benefited from the time off I had with my family," he said. "Maybe it was the fact that we'd won the first half. It seemed that every at-bat was not a do-or-die situation."

The Phillies lost the first two games of the intra-division playoffs to Montreal. Then they rallied and won the next two. But in the fifth and deciding game, Steve Rogers pitched a six-hit shutout and Montreal beat the Phillies, 3–0.

When it was over, manager Dallas Green departed to become general manager of the Chicago Cubs. Green had been critical of the Phillies' mental approach to baseball in the second half of the season.

They had played in spurts, and made fundamental mistakes. But the people in charge had devised a playoff scheme that guaranteed them a spot because they'd been in front when the strike came.

The players, in turn, were bitter about Green's bullying tactics. Schmidt had come in for his share of scorn from Green, even though Mike had won six Gold Glove awards for his fielding.

"I don't think he's as prepared as he thinks he is for playing the game," Green said, referring to Mike's habit of skipping infield practice.

"There's a pattern there, the throwing error in the early innings of a ballgame. It would be better for the team if he took infield practice. If, in fact, he's a true leader, he's got to be out there. Okay, maybe it's surface stuff, but it ties in with being a super-class guy."

Green had recommended Pat Corrales as his successor, and that left coach Bobby Wine seething. Wine had been responsible for much of Green's game strategy for two years. He thought about leaving, but finally agreed to stay on as a coach when the Phillies named Corrales as the new manager.

Corrales was signed to a two-year contract by Bill Giles, who had put together a group of new owners to purchase the club from Ruly Carpenter.

The first order of business for the new owners was to sign Mike Schmidt to a long-term contract rather than risk losing him in the free-agent marketplace when his current contract ran out.

So on December 23 Schmidt agreed to a new six-year deal. His advisers would not reveal the exact value of the contract, but pegged it between $7.5 million and $12.5 million.

They set up a budget for the Schmidts. Included was a "toy fund" based on 25 percent of Mike's earnings from endorsements, personal appearances, and incentive bonuses; if Mike wanted to go on an expensive trip or buy an exotic car, the money could come from there.

The press voiced concern about envy from teammates and the reaction of Philadelphia's notoriously critical fans.

"Our philosophy," Giles explained, "is that you have to take care of four or five key guys like Rose, Schmidt, Steve Carlton, Gary Matthews.

"You have to treat everybody fairly, but we can't afford to lose one of those four guys.

"You always worry about morale. It goes through your mind. But I think you have to take a look at what you think is the best thing for the bottom line. You can't worry about petty jealousy and squabbles."

Schmidt realized that the fans would expect even more of him now that he was earning over a million dollars a year.

"I feel that I'm a sound hitter now," he said. "Fans are going to say, 'Let's see how he plays now, let's see if he tails off.'

"I have a better approach to handle this sort of pressure than I had when I signed my earlier contract. I can't guarantee good years because you can't guarantee anything in baseball.

"I can say one thing. I'm going to be playing as hard as I ever played and doing my best to improve. I'm not going to be satisfied with the level of the game I'm playing now. I'm going to try and get better, not because I make more money, but just because I have that kind of respect for the game."

13

On the Right Track

Mike Schmidt strode into the 1982 season with a new contract, a new manager, new owners, and a new goal.

No one had ever won baseball's Most Valuable Player award three years in a row. But Mike was young enough, strong enough, and eager enough to do it.

On April 13, a raw, windy day at Shea Stadium, Mike went up to face the Mets' Randy Jones, a former Cy Young winner struggling through a comeback. Jones had a tantalizing assortment of pitches that seldom exceeded 83 miles an hour.

Mike looked at the first pitch. It barely nicked the outside corner of the plate for strike one. Then Jones threw an off-speed breaking pitch,

The starting lineup: Mike and his wife, Donna, with Jonathan and Jessica.

aimed again for the outside corner.

Patiently, Schmidt took his short, measured stride into the ball. With his left shoulder tucked in perfectly, he swung smoothly, confident that he could reach the outside pitch and send it whistling into right field.

That's just what happened. He banged the ball into right field, toward the foul pole, where Met outfielder Ellis Valentine would have to chase it down. It looked like a triple possibly, a double for sure.

As the spectators turned from watching Valentine pursue the ball, they gasped in surprise. Schmidt was limping toward first base, clutching at his back with his left hand. He was bent over with pain.

The ball rattled against the fence, 330 feet out, but Schmidt remained scrunched at first base, holding his side and groaning.

He had torn muscles away from his rib cage. The force of his swing had cracked a lower left rib. The season had barely begun and now Mike Schmidt would have to miss a good part of it.

It was weeks before he could swing the bat properly again. And it was almost two months before he could resume his aggressive style of 1981. But he did, and when he did, he caught fire. He blazed through the hot summer months, and by mid-September he was hitting .300. He had 33 homers and 80 RBI's.

With Schmidt sidelined and three-time Cy Young winner Steve Carlton off to an 0-4 start, the Phillies had stumbled through April. But now they were once again in the thick of a pennant race.

Pete Rose was still chirping around the batting cage, pointing at Schmidt and saying, "There's your MVP."

And then, suddenly, Mike's bat went silent. He went 0-for-17 during a home stand that was supposed to provide the Phillies with the chance to gain some ground on the swift, pesky St. Louis Cardinals.

On September 20 Mike broke through the shackles of that slump with a run-scoring single against the Cardinals in the opening game of a vital three-game series.

Carlton pitched a two-hitter, homered, and won the game, 2–0. The Phillies moved into first place by half a game and the huge crowd went home happy.

The next night the Cardinals recaptured first place. And then, in the final game of the series, Mike faced reliever Bruce Sutter in the eighth inning. The bases were loaded and the Phillies trailed by two runs.

Sutter ran a deep count, pitching carefully, and then he threw another of his famous split-fingered fastballs. Schmidt swung hard, but he only got the top half of the ball and rapped a grounder back at Sutter.

Sutter grabbed it and threw to catcher Darrell Porter for the force. Porter whirled and threw to Keith Hernandez at first to double Schmidt. End of inning, end of rally, end of series.

The Cardinals, armed with a game-and-a-half lead, moved on to New York, where they swept a five-game series from the woeful Mets.

By the time the Phillies met the Cardinals again, St. Louis was comfortably in front. The rookies on that Cardinal ballclub who had never been through the raging heat of a pennant race were relaxed and confident.

When the two teams hooked up again, Schmidt was in a 1-for-25 slump. "You can't blame just one man," said manager Pat Corrales. "You can't blame just Mike Schmidt."

"I don't think it's fair to put the load on his shoulders," said Pete Rose. "When we've got guys not swinging the bat, he feels he has to get three hits and hit two out of the ballpark and that puts too much strain on him.

"He's the best player in the league, but if we don't set the table, he can't knock in runs. It's been a team effort. Everybody from top to bottom had chances to knock in runs.

"Schmitty's hot streak got us back in this thing. With any good team, if one or two guys slump, one or two other guys have got to get hot and pick up the pieces."

It was more than one or two guys. The high-powered engines in the Phillies' lineup—Gary Matthews, Mike Schmidt, and Bo Diaz—all went silent at once, hitting a combined 3-for-35 at one point.

But it was Schmidt, two-time MVP, who

took most of the heat as the Cardinals moved five and a half games in front with 13 games left to play.

"If we're going to start winning games," Schmidt said, "we'll have to break out of it offensively and play well. If we don't, we don't deserve to be division champs.

"One thing for sure, the sun is going to come up in the morning. And . . . I'm not going to read the Philadelphia newspapers tomorrow. Or the St. Louis papers."

The St. Louis papers were filled with glowing stories predicting a championship for their team. The Philadelphia papers were a gloomy contrast, analyzing the Phillies' collapse, second-guessing the shuffling of the pitching rotation, and criticizing the poor hitting of Matthews, Schmidt, and Diaz.

Schmidt never broke out of that slump, and the Cardinals clinched the title with four games left in the season.

Mike's final statistics were solid, if unspectacular. He hit .280, with 35 homers and 87 runs batted in. Only Dave Kingman (37) and Dale Murphy (36) had more homers in 1982. Schmidt led the National League in slugging percentage at .547 and in walks with 107. That meant he was getting on base .403 percent of the time. He also scored 108 runs. Still, he had not played up to the standards he had set for himself.

"I'm looking forward to next year," he said solemnly. "I'll work even harder.

"I look at what I achieved this year, the things I accomplished in only three good months. I can't help wondering what kind of numbers I can put on the board if I put six good months together."

Strangers wondered how Schmidt could take such a disappointing finish so calmly. They did not know the depths of his faith, the sequence of his rearranged priorities.

"I enjoy life," he explained patiently, "even if I'm hitting .245. I'm not going to let my life be run by what I do on the field."

He could not have said that in 1973, after his wretched .196 season.

"He has gone from the boy of twenty-four to the man of thirty-three," Donna Schmidt said. "There was the natural aging, becoming more mature, but it's more than that. His priorities have changed."

The Schmidts' lifestyle had changed too. But not as dramatically as people might think. The handsome couple had moved into a French-style mansion in suburban Media, Pennsylvania, with their two children, Jessica, four, and Jonathan, two. But there were no priceless paintings on the walls, no $400 bottles of wine in the climate-controlled cellar, no Rolls-Royces in the driveway.

"I remember that first winter in Puerto Rico," Donna Schmidt said. "I was afraid to ask Michael for money for hair spray. Not because he wouldn't have given it to me, but because I was used to supporting myself.

"And then he would go out and buy an onyx chess set. We couldn't even play with it, because it hurt our eyes.

"But now we don't buy jewelry. Michael has his Porsche, which I will not attempt to drive. But we haven't rushed out to buy a lot of extravagant things.

"Michael wants a greenhouse. That is his big obsession. He loves to plant flowers in the summertime. He is always working outdoors.

"He is what they call a *fimpster* in Danish. That means someone who tinkers with things, constantly adjusting them. He will rearrange the bedcovers thirty times on the kids, even when they are sound asleep.

"He is an amazing father. The kids love it when he's around. He does neat things. And he is so patient. He got up for those early morning feedings, he changed diapers, he baby-sat. He is wonderful with the kids."

Mike Schmidt is not only wonderfully patient with his own kids, but is deeply concerned about all kids. He devoted considerable time and energy, along with Larry Bowa and Garry Maddox, to raising funds for the Child Guidance Clinic in Philadelphia, a center designed to help troubled families.

He joined forces with actress Sally Struthers of *All in the Family* fame to support the Christian Children's Fund.

"I saw one of her ads in a magazine," Mike said. "I was flying somewhere. All of a sudden bells started ringing. I thought this was something major-league players could get involved in, just as the football players are involved in United Way.

"I wrote a letter, offered to help, checked them out. Now I'm sponsoring a little girl in Teculatan, which is in Guatemala. Her name is Marta. She almost died from malnutrition. Now they have a nutrition center in her town and at least once a day she can go there for a balanced meal.

"The fifteen-dollar-a-month support check seemed so little. What I have is the vision of having someone growing up, having a successful life, maybe meeting her somewhere, sometime."

With all Mike's fame came a deeper sense of responsibility. "I'd like to leave a mark," he said in the spring of 1982. "A mark by example. Grade-school kids are experiencing now what I didn't experience until college. If a kid in the eighth grade has run the gamut of experiences from sex to drugs to liquor, if he's gotten in the habit of altering his state of mind as often as he can, is he going to grow out of that by the time he's twenty?

"When I was growing up I followed the crowd. That's why it bothers me to go to schools and see there's no respect for hygiene, no respect for the way you look, no respect for teachers, no respect for the mind. There's only respect for whoever has the most fun."

Mike has always been a team player who never hesitated to acknowledge those who helped him along the way: his father, the strict disciplinarian; his Little League coach, Jack Fenner; his high school coach, Dave Palsgrove; and his Ohio University coach, Bob Wren.

Later there was Tony Lucadello, the scout who signed him; Andy Seminick, the former Phillie catcher who encouraged him in the minors; Cal Emery, who worked with him daily one season; and Danny Ozark, who wanted him to succeed so badly.

Mike prizes the friendship of Dave Cash, who brought a winning attitude to the Phillies;

Dick Allen, who took a special interest in him; and Pete Rose, who has been a constant inspiration.

Mike has been an MVP, a home-run champ, and a member of a World Series championship team, but as he entered the 1983 season there were still goals to achieve.

"Before I'm through I'd like to play a hundred and sixty-two games in a season and I'd like to get a hundred at-bats in World Series competition," he said.

Summers, he plays hard. Winters, he often retreats to his attic, where he has an elaborate model-train layout, complete with scenery, people, and buildings. These are metal miniature trains, accurate in every respect. The trains whistle, the lights blink, the little red caboose brings up the rear.

"I had a layout as a little boy," Mike said. "One day I saw some model trains on sale, so I started collecting. And now I like to come up here when the weather turns cold.

"I like to arrange the tracks in different configurations. I like the idea of making the trains stop where I want them to, when I want them to."

Mike Schmidt is in control. Of his trains. Of his career. Of his life.

About the Author

Stan Hochman has been a sports columnist for the Philadelphia *Daily News* for twenty-four years. He was born in Brooklyn, New York, and earned his Bachelor and Master of Arts degrees from New York University. Mr. Hochman started his career as a history teacher in the Brooklyn public schools. He went on to write sports for newspapers in Texas and California.

The author has won many awards for writing, including the Pro Football Writers and U.S. Basketball Writers competitions and the 1983 National Headlines Award. His columns have appeared in *Best Sports Stories* thirteen times. This is his first work for young readers.